Piano · Vocal · Guitar

Classic Coffeehouse Hits

61 Choice Songs

W9-BGS-913

Cover Photo by Chris Jensen
Photo Courtesy of Java Joe's Coffee & Espresso (Ventura, California)

ISBN 978-0-634-02239-5

CREATIVE CONCEPTS
PUBLISHING

EXCLUSIVELY DISTRIBUTED BY

HAL·LEONARD®
CORPORATION
7777 W. BLUEMOUND RD. P.O. BOX 13819 MILWAUKEE, WI 53213

Visit Hal Leonard Online at
www.halleonard.com

CONTENTS

ABRAHAM, MARTIN AND JOHN

Words and Music by
RICHARD HOLLER

6

AN AMERICAN TRILOGY

Words and Music by
MICKEY NEWBURY

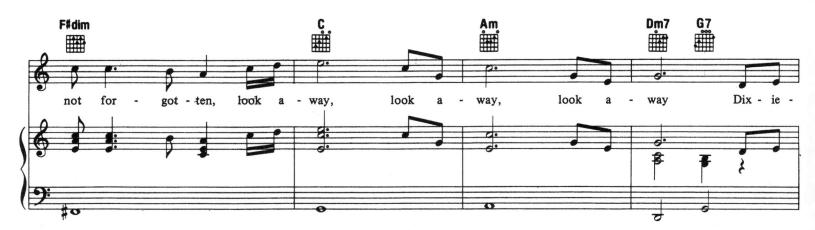

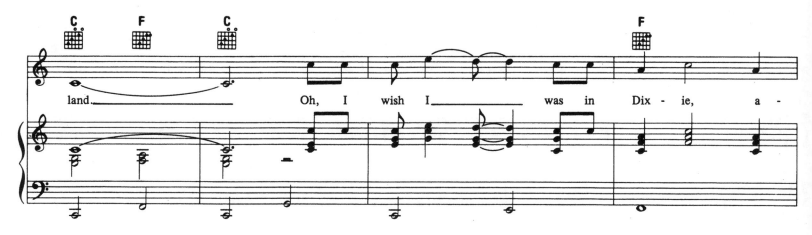

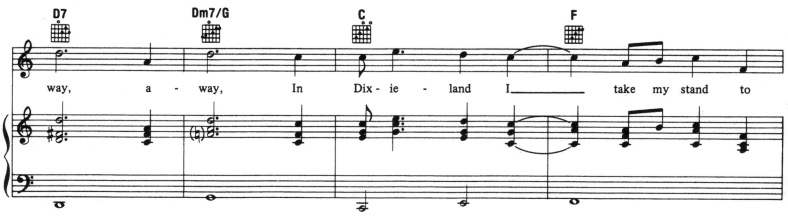

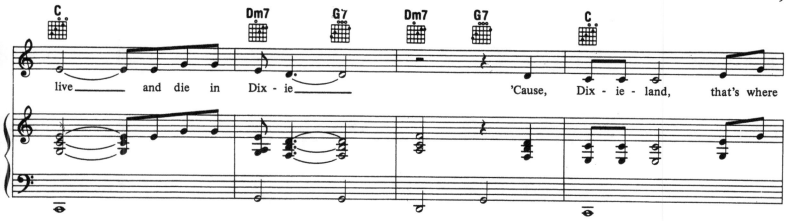

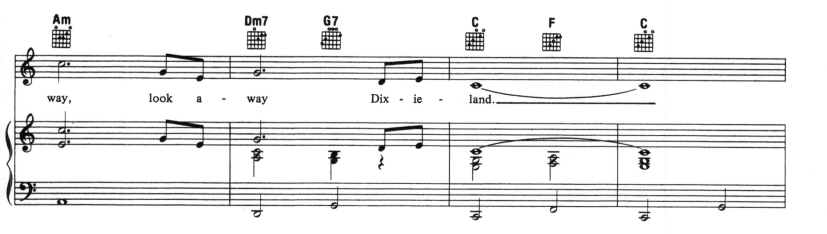

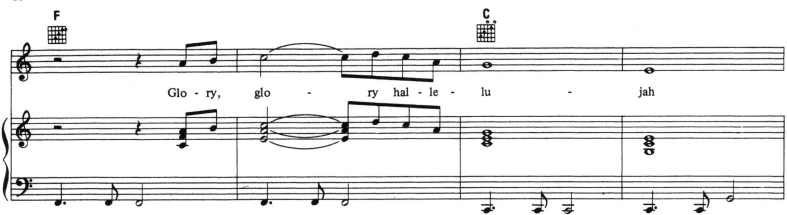

Glo - ry, glo - ry hal - le - lu - jah

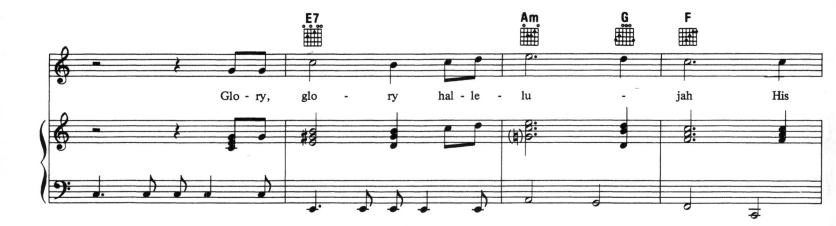

Glo - ry, glo - ry hal - le - lu - jah His

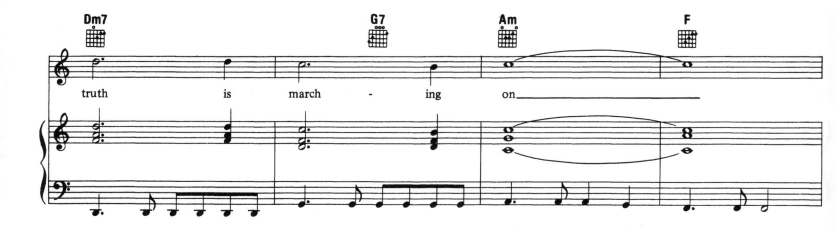

truth is march - ing on

So hush, lit - tle chil - dren,

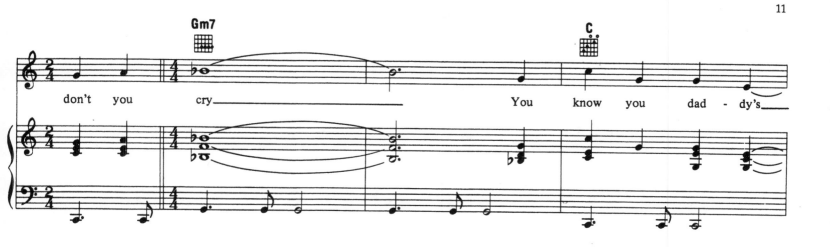

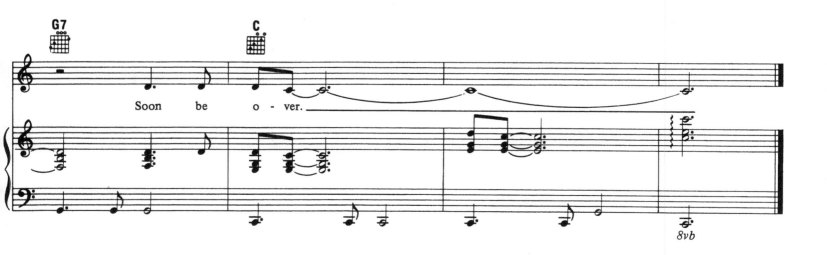

AMIE

By CRAIG FULLER

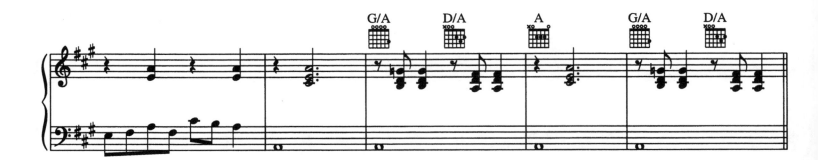

13

thought that I ___ might ___ keep you for ___ my ___ own. _____
nev - er see ___ what's ___ right or what ___ is ___ wrong. _____

one of us, ___ I'm ___ sure we both ___ will ___ see. _____

___ *(Spoken:) It'd take too long to see.*

Solo ends

___ *(Spoken:) Oh, won't you look at me and tell me?*

A - mie, _____ what you wan - na do? _____

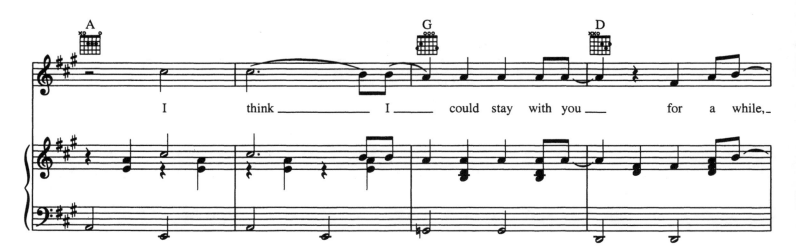

I ___ think _____ I ___ could stay with you ___ for a while,

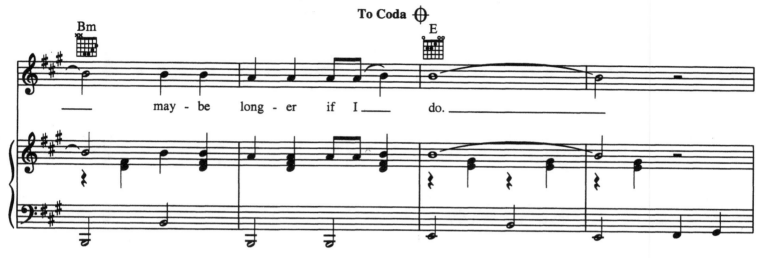

may - be long - er if I ____ do. ____

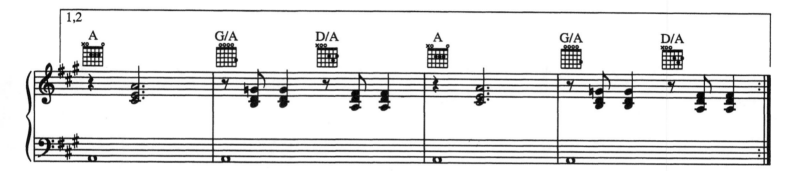

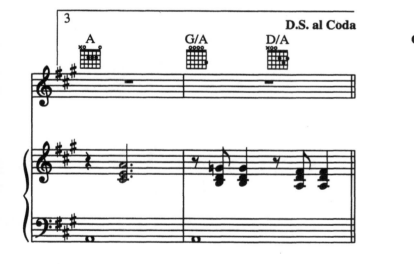

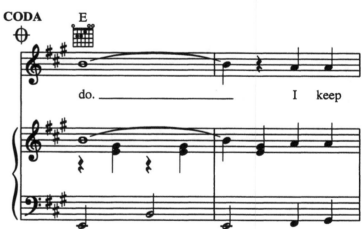

do. ____ I keep

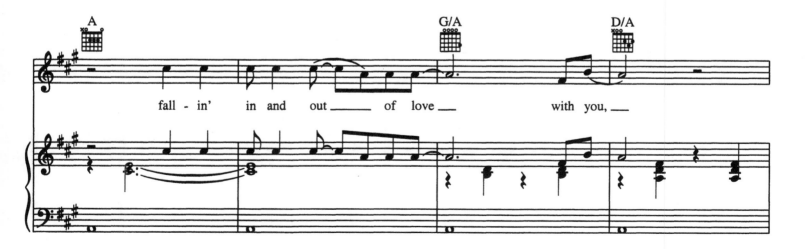

fall - in' in and out ____ of love ____ with you, ____

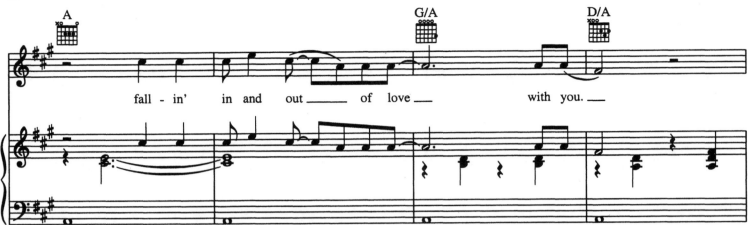

fall - in' in and out ___ of love ___ with you. ___

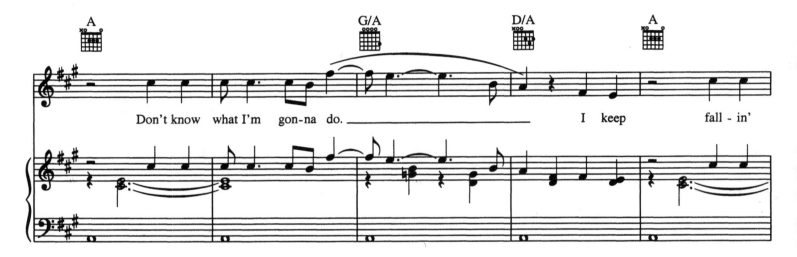

Don't know what I'm gon-na do. ___ I keep fall - in'

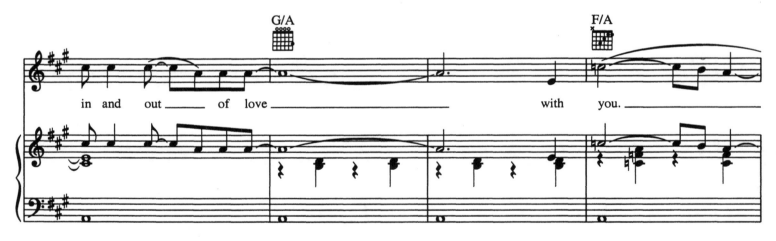

in and out ___ of love ___ with you. ___

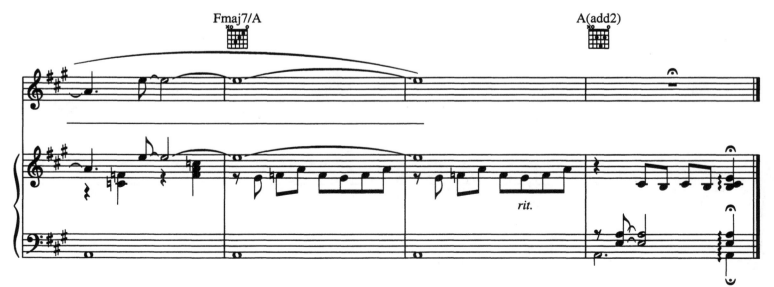

rit.

ANGEL OF THE MORNING

Words and Music by
CHIP TAYLOR

There'll be no strings to bind your hands,___ not if my love can't bind your
May-be the sun's light will be dim,___ and it won't mat-ter an-y-

heart;
how;

and there's no need to take a
if morn-ing's ech-o says we've

stand___ for it was I who chose to start.
sinned, well, it was what I want-ed now.

18

19

I won't beg you to stay with me,___ through the tears

of the day,___ of the years.

Ba - by,___ ba-by, ba - by   Just call me an - gel___ of the

Repeat and Fade

morn - ing,___ (an - gel)   just touch my cheek be - fore you leave me,   ba - by.

BIG BAD JOHN

Words and Music by
JIMMY DEAN

Verse 1. Every morning at the mine you could see him arrive,
He stood six-foot-six and weighed two-forty-five.
Kind of broad at the shoulder and narrow at the hip,
And everybody knew you didn't give no lip to Big John!
(Refrain)

Verse 2. Nobody seemed to know where John called home,
He just drifted into town and stayed all alone.
He didn't say much, a-kinda quiet and shy,
And if you spoke at all, you just said, "Hi" to Big John!
Somebody said he came from New Orleans,
Where he got in a fight over a Cajun queen.
And a crashing blow from a huge right hand
Sent a Louisiana fellow to the promised land. Big John!
(Refrain)

Verse 3. Then came the day at the bottom of the mine
When a timber cracked and the men started crying.
Miners were praying and hearts beat fast,
And everybody thought that they'd breathed their last 'cept John.
Through the dust and the smoke of this man-made hell
Walked a giant of a man that the miners knew well.
Grabbed a sagging timber and gave out with a groan,
And, like a giant oak tree, just stood there alone. Big John!
(Refrain)

Verse 4. And with all of his strength, he gave a mighty shove;
Then a miner yelled out, "There's a light up above!"
And twenty men scrambled from a would-be grave,
And now there's only one left down there to save; Big John!
With jacks and timbers they started back down
Then came that rumble way down in the ground,
And smoke and gas belched out of that mine,
Everybody knew it was the end of the line for Big John!
(Refrain)

Verse 5. Now they never re-opened that worthless pit,
They just placed a marble stand in front of it;
These few words are written on that stand:
"At the bottom of this mine lies a big, big man; Big John!"
(Refrain)

BLACKBIRD

Words and Music by JOHN LENNON
and PAUL McCARTNEY

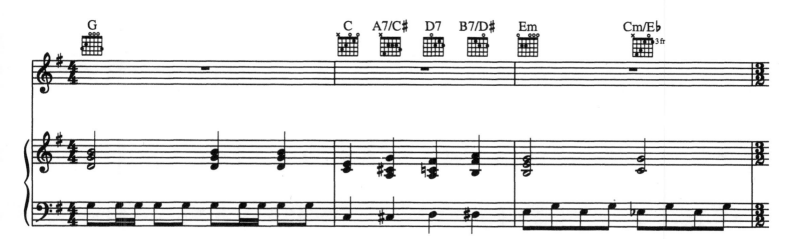

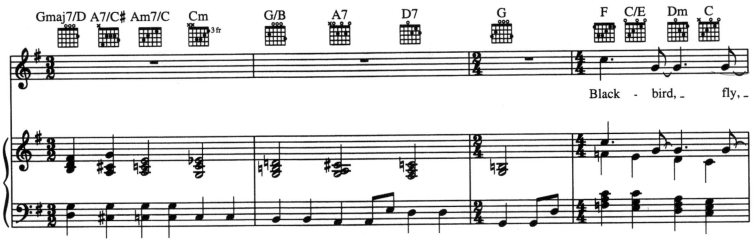

Black - bird, fly,

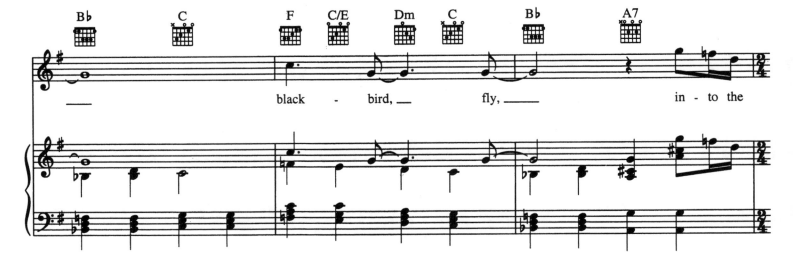

black - bird, fly, in - to the

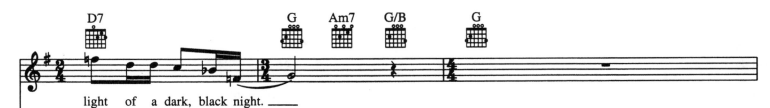

light of a dark, black night.

molto rit.

a tempo

BRAND NEW KEY

Words and Music by
MELANIE SAFKA

get to - geth - er and try them out, __ you see. __

F

I been look - ing a - round a - while, _ you got some - thing for

C

me.   Oh, I got a brand new pair of roll - er skates,

Last time Repeat and Fade

you got a brand new key. _____

COTTON FIELDS
(The Cotton Song)

Words and Music by
HUDDIE LEDBETTER

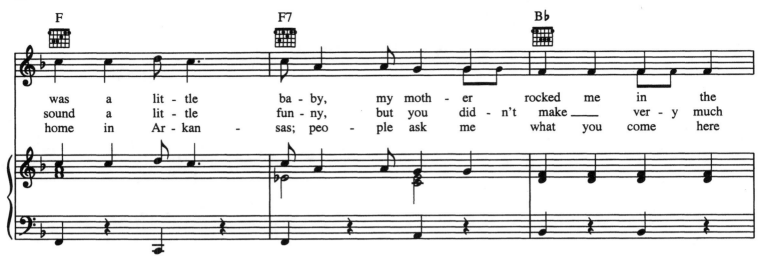

was a lit - tle ba - by, my moth - er rocked me in the
sound a lit - tle fun - ny, but you did - n't make ___ ver - y much
home in Ar - kan - sas; peo - ple ask me what you come here

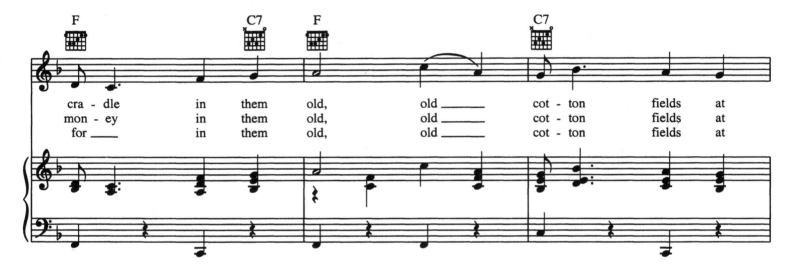

cra - dle in them old, old _____ cot - ton fields at
mon - ey in them old, old _____ cot - ton fields at
for ___ in them old, old _____ cot - ton fields at

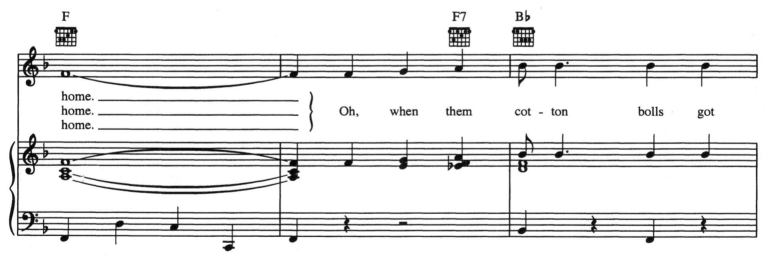

home. _____
home. _____
home. _____ Oh, when them cot - ton bolls got

rot - ten you could - n't pick ver - y much cot - ton in them old

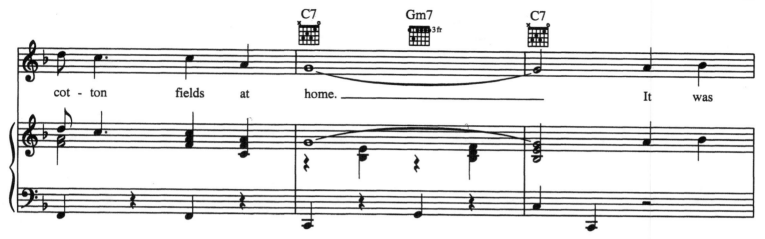

cot - ton fields at home. _____ It was

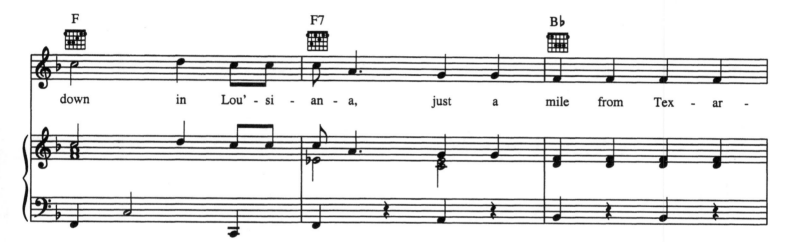

down in Lou' - si - an - a, just a mile from Tex - ar -

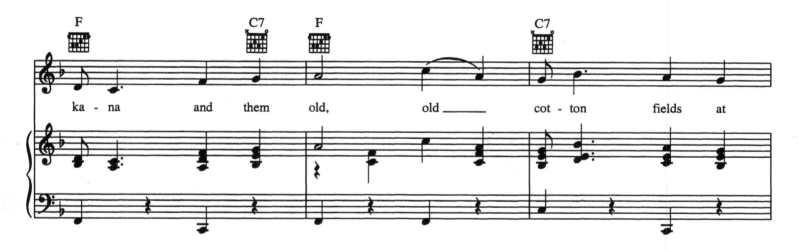

ka - na and them old, old _____ cot - ton fields at

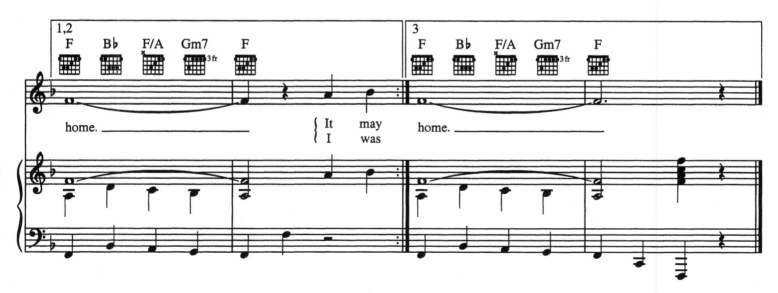

home. _____ It may / I was

home. _____

CATCH THE WIND

Words and Music by
DONOVAN LEITCH

1. In the chil - ly hours and
(Verses 2 & 3 see block lyric)

mi - nutes of un - cer - tain - ty.

I want to be in the warm hold of your

lov - ing mind. To

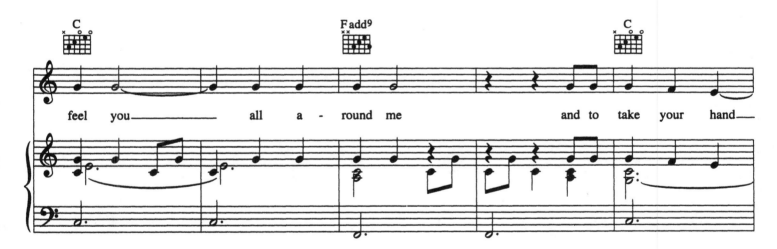

feel you _____ all a - round me and to take your hand _____

_____ a - long the sand, ah, but I may as well

⊕ *Coda*

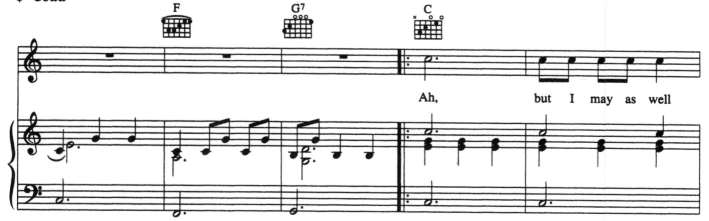

Ah,   but I may as well

ad lib. to fade

try   and   catch   the   wind.

Verse 2:
When sundown pales the sky
I want to hide awhile
Behind your smile
And everywhere I'd look, your eyes I'd find.

For me to love you now
Would be the sweetest thing
'Twould make me sing
Ah but I may as well try and catch the wind.

Verse 3:
When rain has hung the leaves with tears
I want you near
To kill my fears
To help me leave all my blues behind

For standing in your heart
Is where I want to be
And I long to be
Ah but I may as well try and catch the wind.

DAYDREAM

Words and Music by
JOHN SEBASTIAN

3. *Whistle*
   Whistle
   Whistle
   Whistle
   And you can be sure that if you're feelin' right,
   A daydream will last till long into the night.
   Tomorrow at breakfast you may pick up your ears,
   Or you may be daydreamin' for a thousand years.

DON'T LET ME BE LONELY TONIGHT

Words and Music by
JAMES TAYLOR

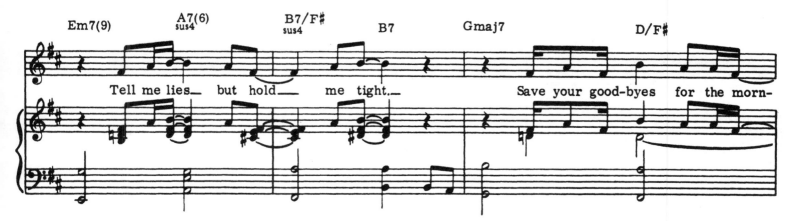

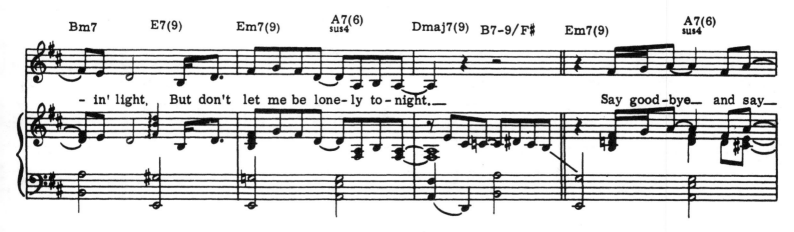

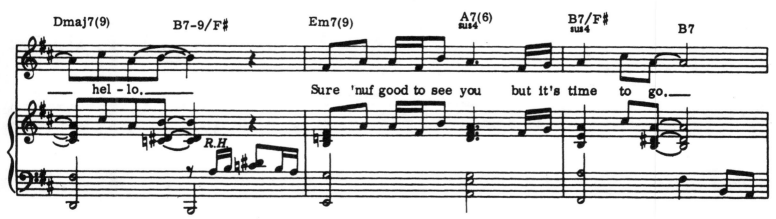

Don't say yes, but please don't say no,___ I don't want to be lone-ly to-night.___

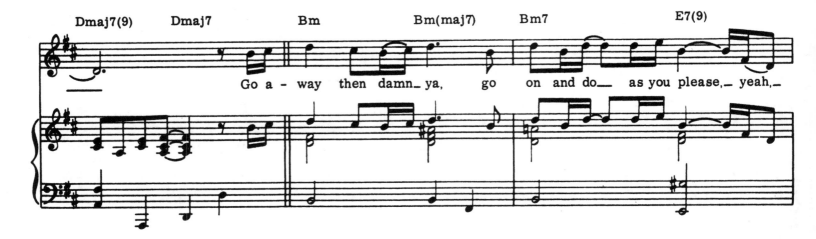

Go a-way then damn_ya, go on and do__ as you please,_ yeah,_

You ain't gon-na see me get-tin' down on my knees._ I'm un-de-cid-ed and

your heart's been_di-vid-ed, you've been turn-in' my world_ up-side down.___

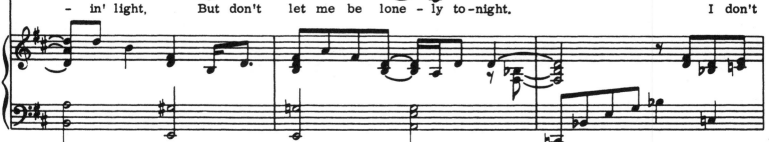

DON'T LET THE RAIN COME DOWN

(Crooked Little Man) (Crooked Little House)

Words and Music by ERSEL HICKY
and ED E. MILLER

44

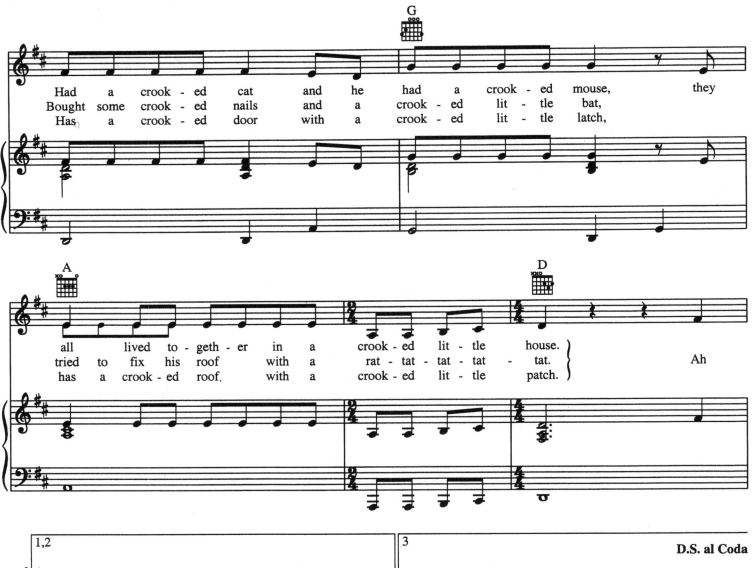

Had a crook-ed cat and he had a crook-ed mouse, they
Bought some crook-ed nails and a crook-ed lit-tle bat,
Has a crook-ed door with a crook-ed lit-tle latch,

all lived to-geth-er in a crook-ed lit-tle house.
tried to fix his roof with a rat-tat-tat-tat-tat.
has a crook-ed roof, with a crook-ed lit-tle patch.

Ah

D.S. al Coda

hah, oh no. Don't let the hah, oh no. Don't let the

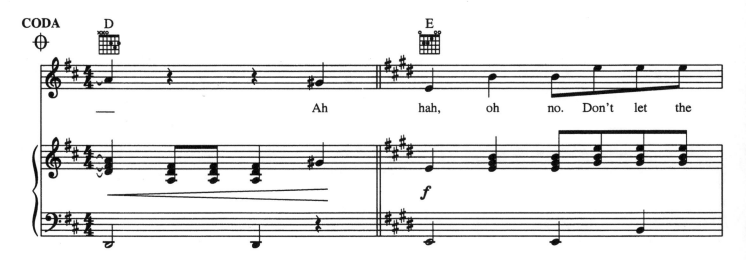

CODA

Ah hah, oh no. Don't let the

rain come down. _ Ah hah, oh no. Don't let the rain come down. _ Ah

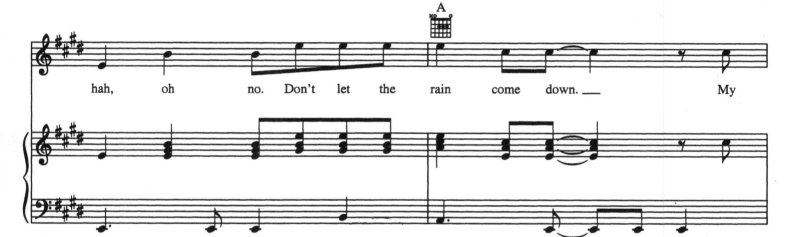

hah, oh no. Don't let the rain come down. ___ My

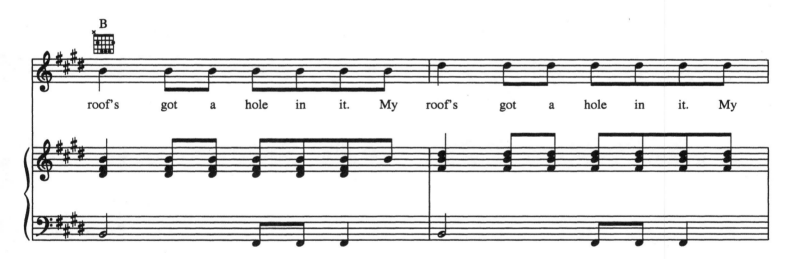

roof's got a hole in it. My roof's got a hole in it. My

roof's got a hole in it and I might drown.

DUST IN THE WIND

Words and Music by
KERRY LIVGREN

Moderate Folk style

Dust   in the wind.
Dust   in the wind.

All they are ___ is dust in ___ the wind.

All we are ___ is dust in ___ the wind. ___

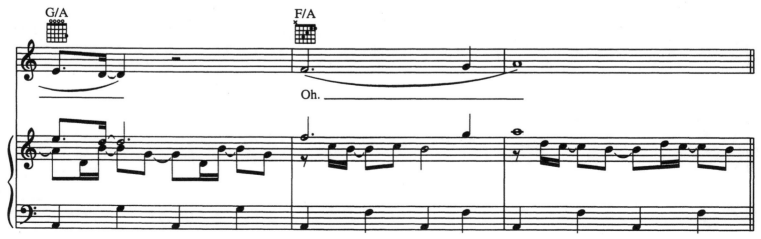

___   Oh. ___

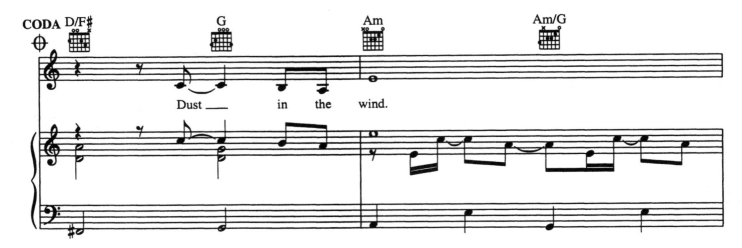

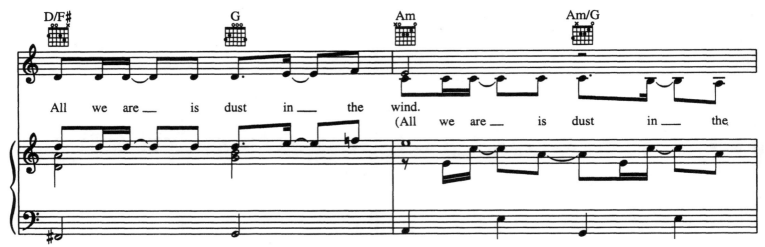

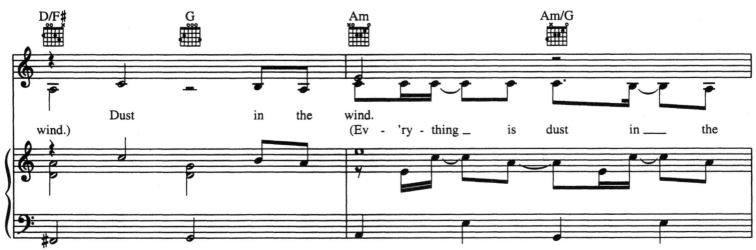

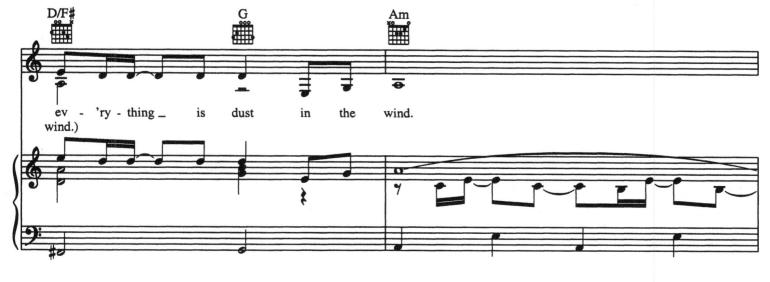

ev - 'ry - thing _ is dust in the wind.
wind.)

Repeat and Fade

Optional Ending

poco rit.

FIRE AND RAIN

Words and Music by
JAMES TAYLOR

Slowly

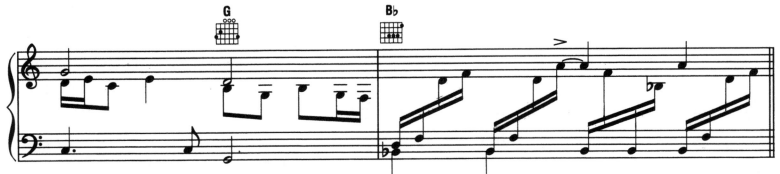

Verses 1&2:

Just yes-ter-day morn-ing they let me know__ you were gone__
Look down up-on me, Je-sus, you've got to help me make a stand__

Su - san the plans they made put an end to you
You've just got to see me through an - oth - er day

THE FIRST TIME
EVER I SAW YOUR FACE

Words and Music by
EWAN MacCOLL

Slowly

Pedal throughout

The First_ Time _____ Ev-er I Saw Your Face,_____

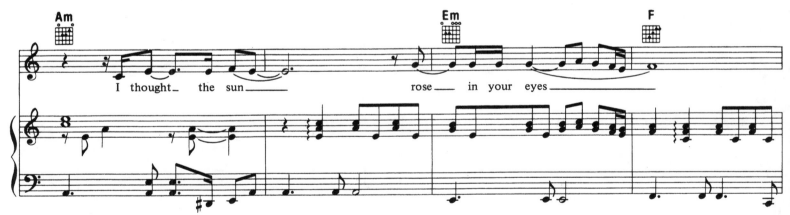

I thought_ the sun_____ rose____ in your eyes _____

To Coda

And the moon____ and the stars _____ were the gifts you gave____ To_

FIVE HUNDRED MILES

Words and Music by
HEDY WEST

Moderately slow

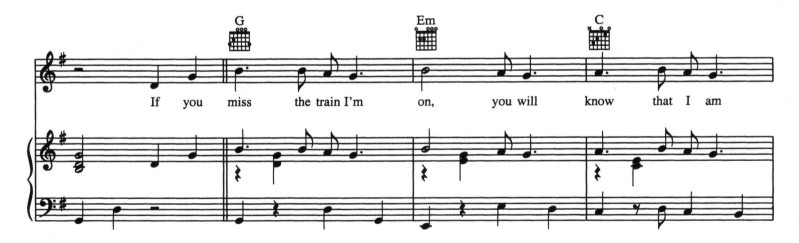

If you miss the train I'm on, you will know that I am

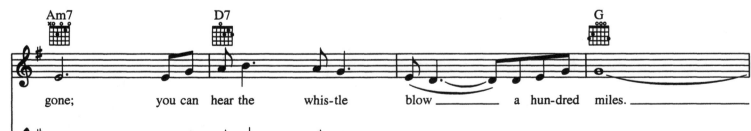

gone; you can hear the whis-tle blow _____ a hun-dred miles. _____

home, a-way from home, a-way from home, a-way from home, Lord, I'm
way, this-a-way, this-a-way, this-a-way, Lord, I

five __ hun-dred miles __ a-way from home. __ Not a
can't __ go back home __ this-a-

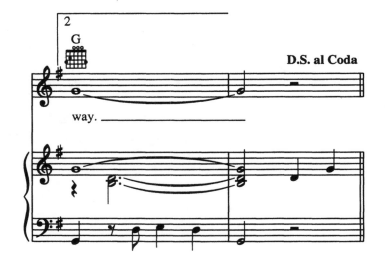

way. __

D.S. al Coda

CODA

You can hear the whis-tle

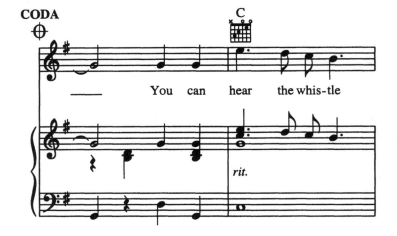

rit.

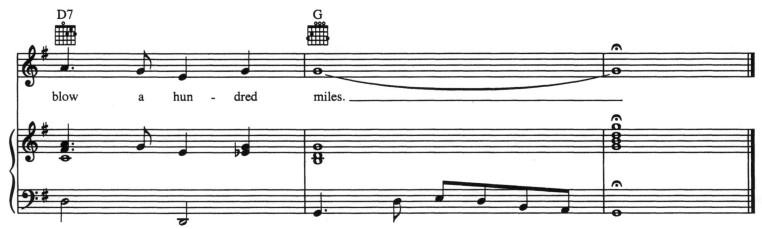

blow a hun-dred miles. __

THE FOOL ON THE HILL

Words and Music by JOHN LENNON
and PAUL McCARTNEY

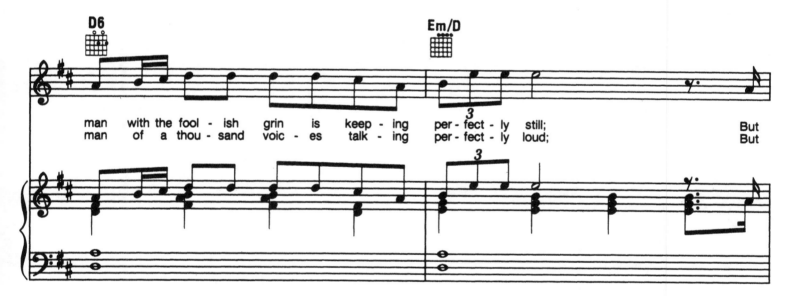

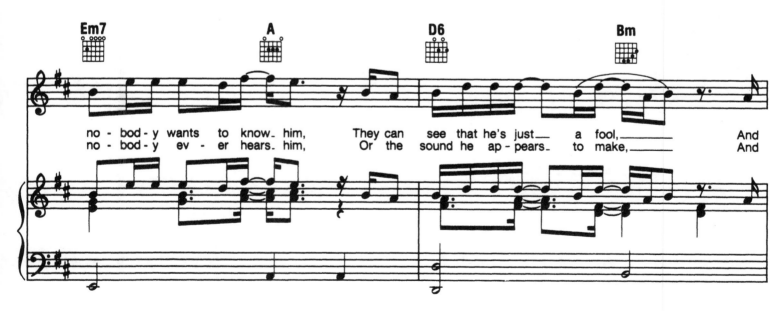

62

GOTTA TRAVEL ON

Words and Music by PAUL CLAYTON, LARRY EHRLICH,
DAVID LAZAR and TOM SIX

HAPPY TOGETHER

Words and Music by GARRY BONNER
and ALAN GORDON

68

HE AIN'T HEAVY...
HE'S MY BROTHER

Words and Music by BOB RUSSELL
and BOBBY SCOTT

Moderately slow, with feeling

with pedal throughout

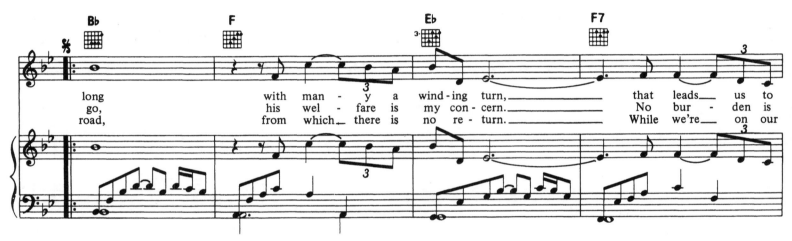

| Bb | F | Eb | F7 |

long / go, / road,
with man-y a wind-ing turn, / that leads us to
his wel-fare is my con-cern. / No bur-den is
from which there is no re-turn. / While we're on our

| Gm | Ab | F11 |

who / he / way
knows where, / who knows where. / But I'm
to bear, / we'll get there. / For
to there, / why not share? / And the

| Bbmaj7 | F | Eb |

strong, / know / load
strong e-nough to car-ry him. / He Ain't
he would not en-cum-ber me. / He Ain't
does-n't weigh me down at all. / He Ain't

HERE COMES THE SUN

Words and Music by
GEORGE HARRISON

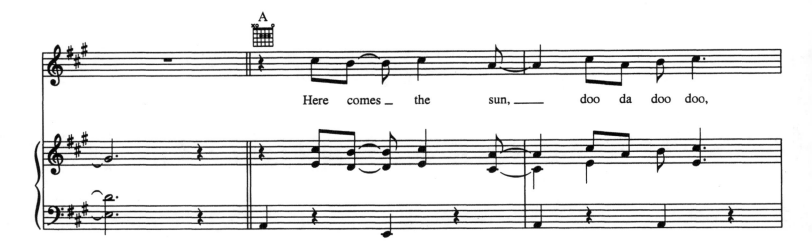

Here comes _ the sun, ___ doo da doo doo,

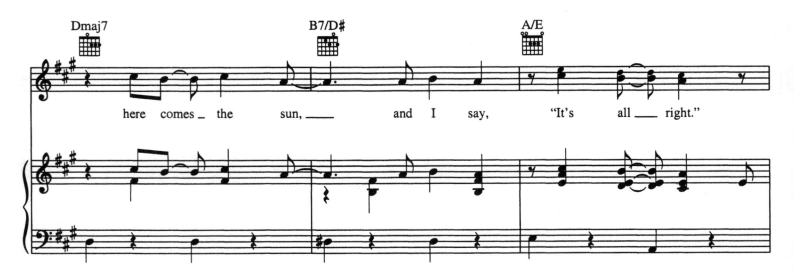

here comes _ the sun, ___ and I say, "It's all ___ right."

Lit - tle dar - ling,
Lit - tle dar - ling,
Lit - tle dar - ling,

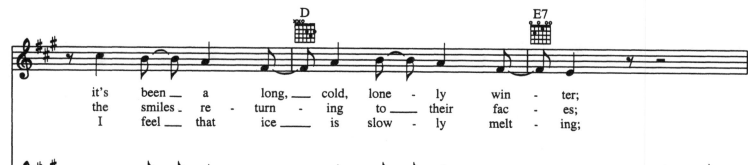

it's been ___ a long, ___ cold, lone - ly win - ter;
the smiles ___ re - turn - ing to ___ their fac - es;
I feel ___ that ice ___ is slow - ly melt - ing;

lit - tle dar - ling, it feels ___ like years ___ since it's ___ been here.
lit - tle dar - ling, it seems ___ like years ___ since it's ___ been here.
lit - tle dar - ling, it seems ___ like years ___ since it's ___ been clear. ___

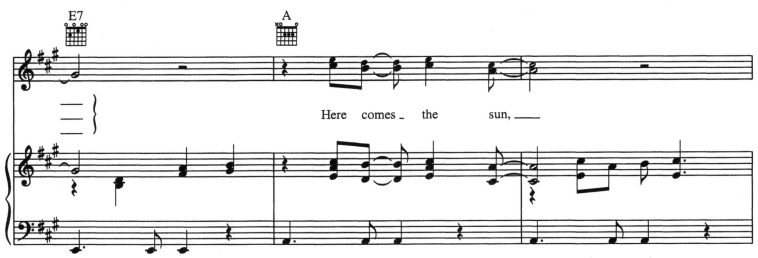

Here comes ___ the ___ sun, ___

here comes ___ the ___ sun, ___ and I say, "It's all ___ right."

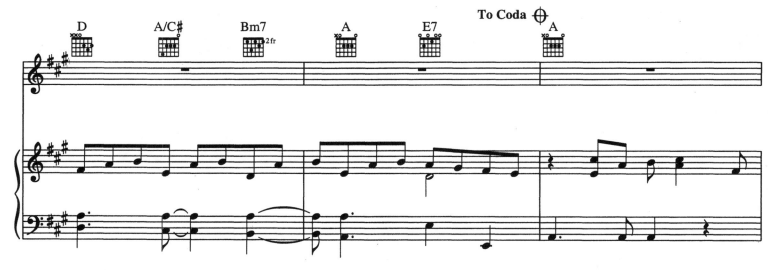

To Coda ⊕

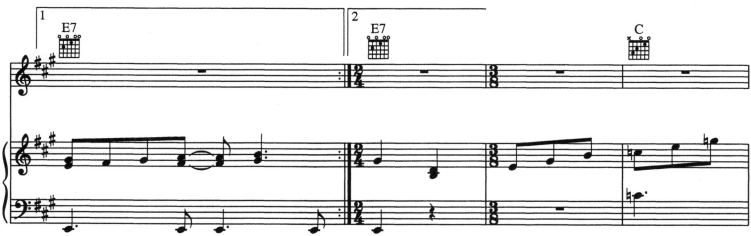

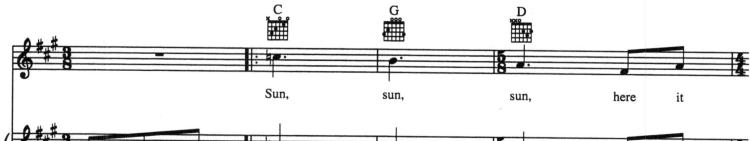

Sun, sun, sun, here it

comes.

D.S. al Coda

76

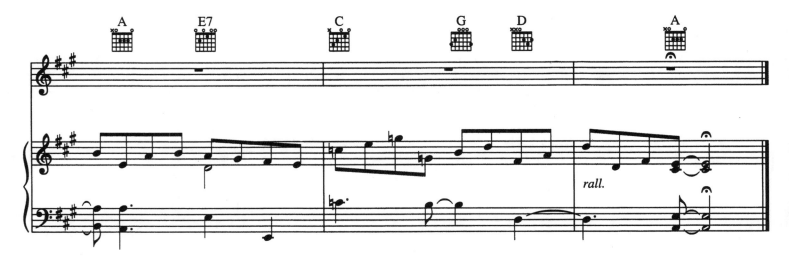

I'LL NEVER FIND ANOTHER YOU

Words and Music by
TOM SPRINGFIELD

78

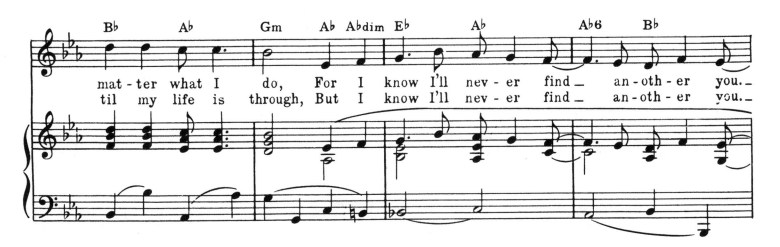

matter what I do, For I know I'll nev-er find _ an-oth-er you. _
til my life is through, But I know I'll nev-er find _ an-oth-er you. _

There is

It's a

long, long jour-ney, So stay by my side; When I

walk through the storm you'll be my guide. _ If they

THE HUNGRY YEARS

Words and Music by NEIL SEDAKA
and HOWARD GREENFIELD

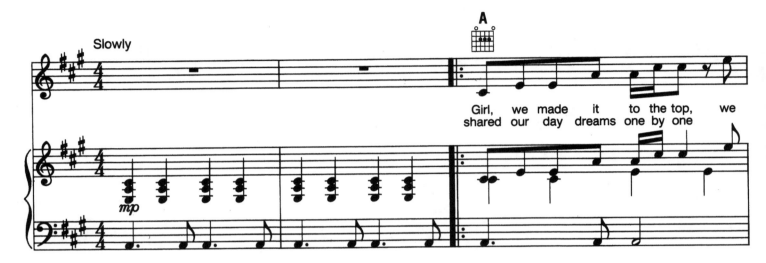

Slowly

Girl, we made it to the top, we
shared our day dreams one by one

went so high we could-n't stop, we climbed the lad-der lead-ing us no-
mak-ing plans was so much fun; we set our goals and reached the high-est

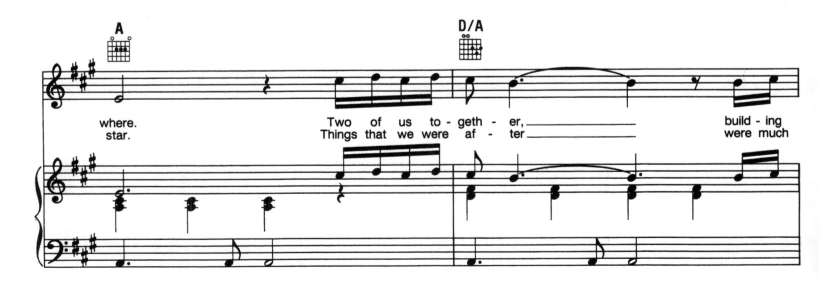

where. Two of us to-geth-er, build-ing
star. Things that we were af-ter were much

I FEEL THE EARTH MOVE

Words and Music by
CAROLE KING

Ooh, _ dar - lin', _ when you're near _ me _ and you ten -

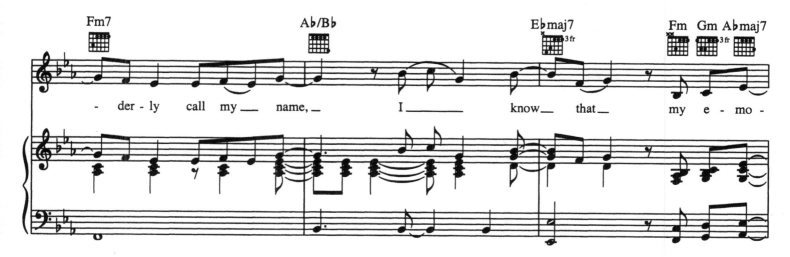

- der - ly call my _ name, _ I _ know _ that _ my e - mo -

- tions are some - thing I just _ can't tame. _ I've just got to have _ you, _

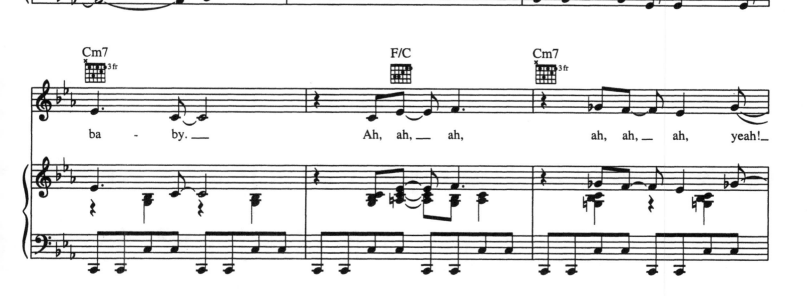

ba - by. _ Ah, ah, _ ah, ah, ah, _ ah, yeah! _

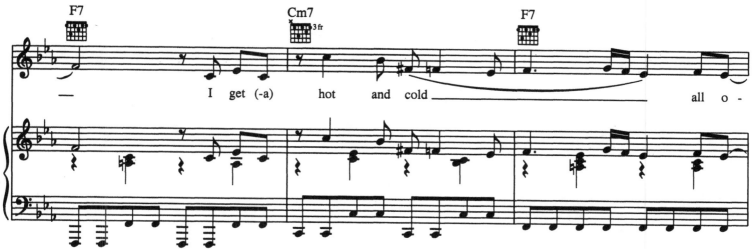

I get (-a) hot and cold _____ all o-

D.S. al Coda

-ver, all o- ver, all o- ver, all o-ver. I feel the

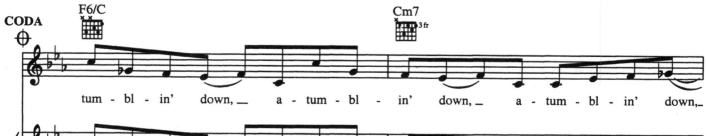

CODA

tum-bl-in' down, ___ a-tum-bl-in' down, ___ a-tum-bl-in' down, ___

rit.

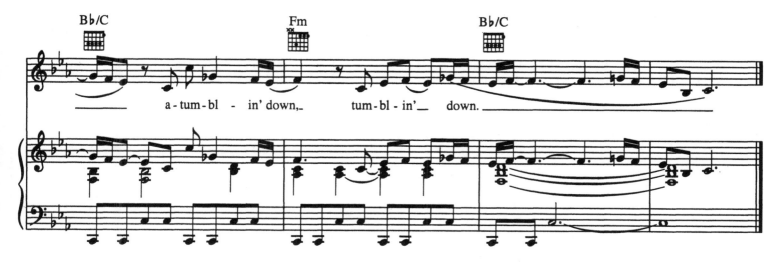

_____ a-tum-bl-in' down, ___ tum-bl-in' ___ down. _____

I FOUGHT THE LAW

Words and Music by
SONNY CURTIS

IF

Words and Music by
DAVID GATES

Moderately, with feeling

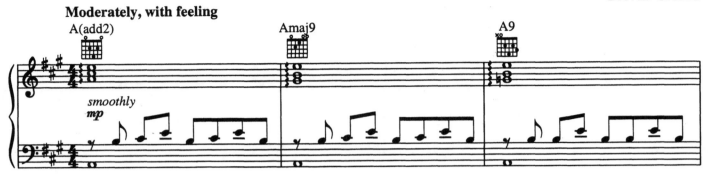

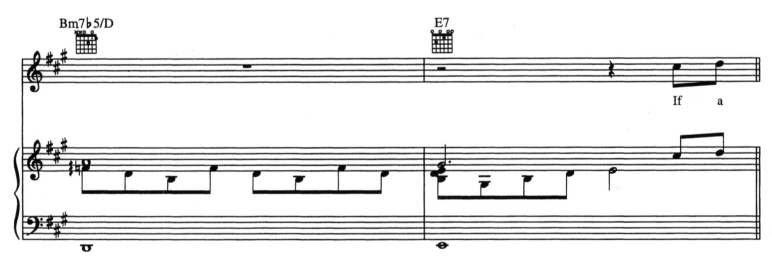

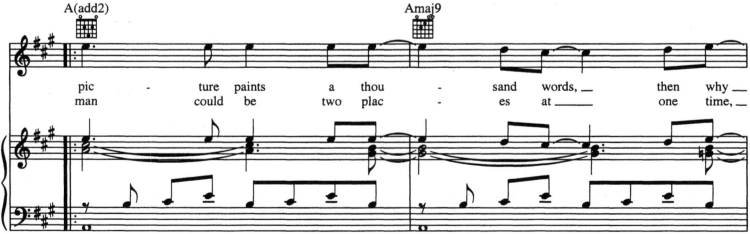

pic - ture paints a thou - sand words, __ then why
man could be a two plac - es at __ one time, __

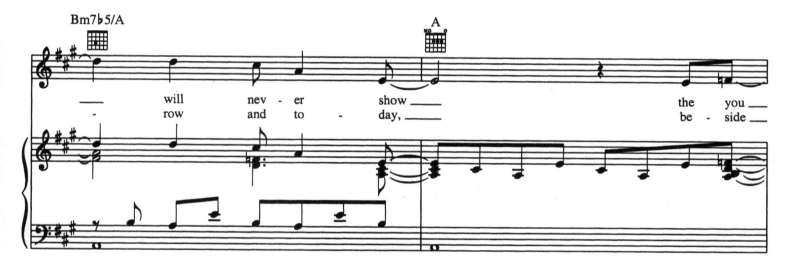

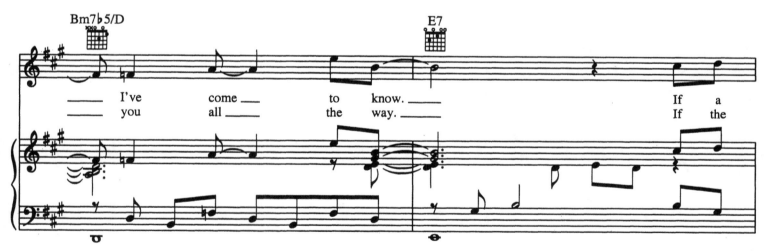

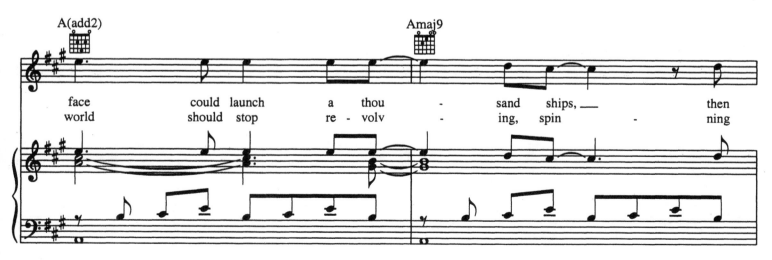

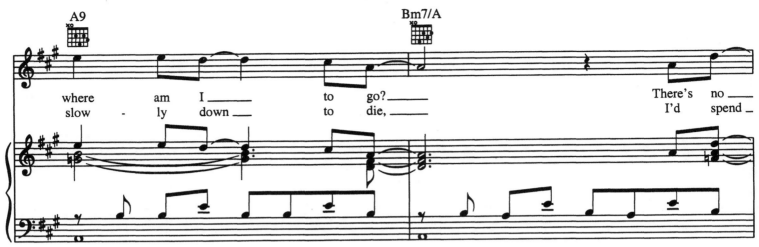

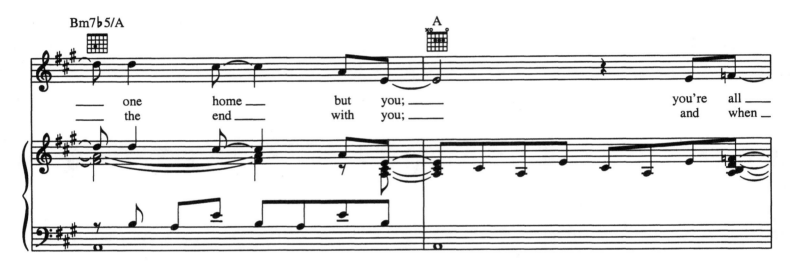

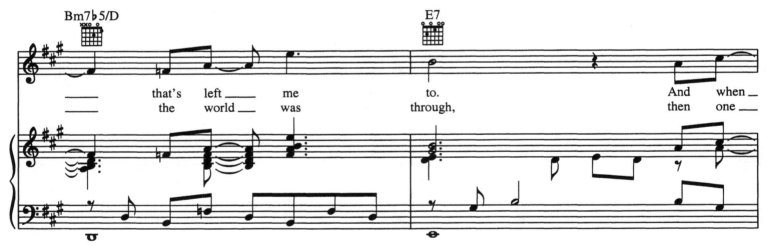

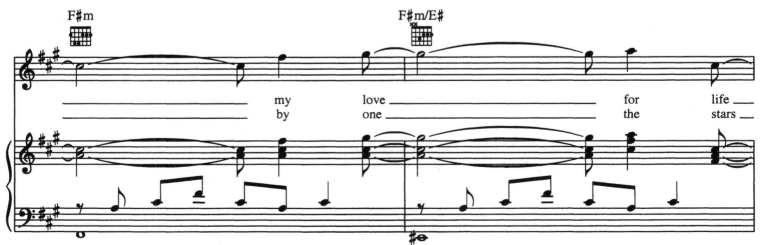

IF I HAD A HAMMER
(The Hammer Song)

Words and Music by LEE HAYS
and PETE SEEGER

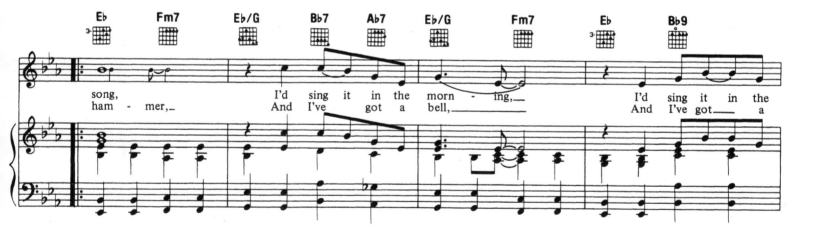

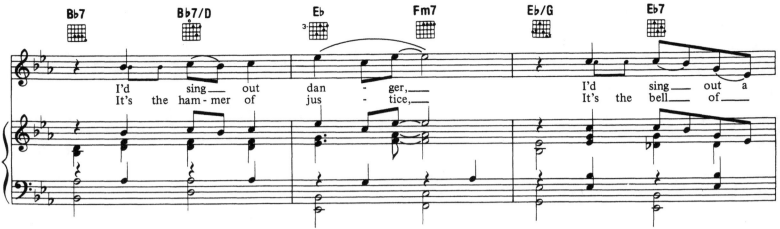

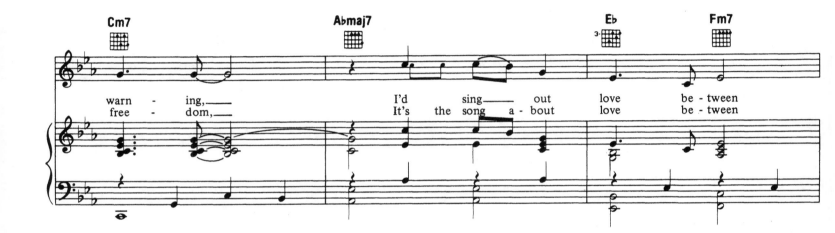

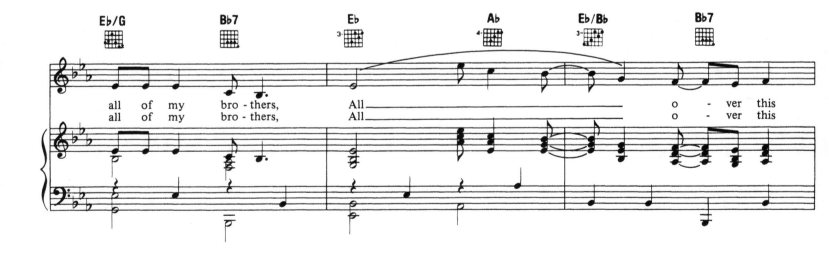

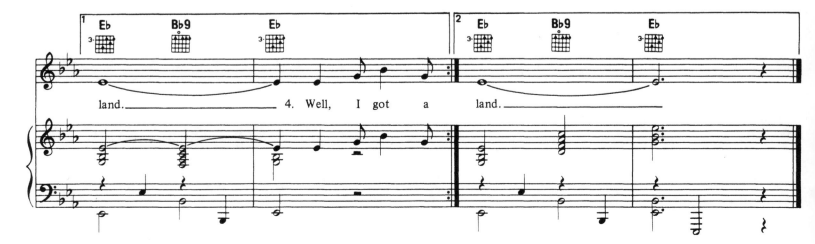

IN MY LIFE

Words and Music by JOHN LENNON
and PAUL McCARTNEY

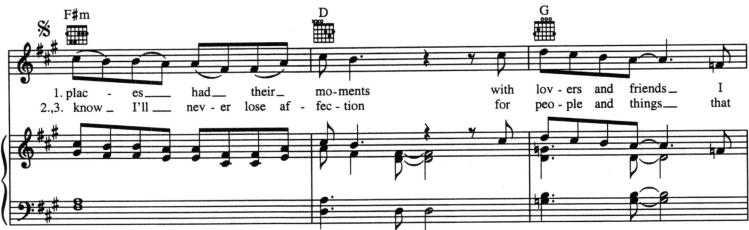

1. plac - es____ had____ their__ mo-ments with lov-ers and friends__ I
2.,3. know__ I'll____ nev-er lose af - fec - tion for peo - ple and things__ that

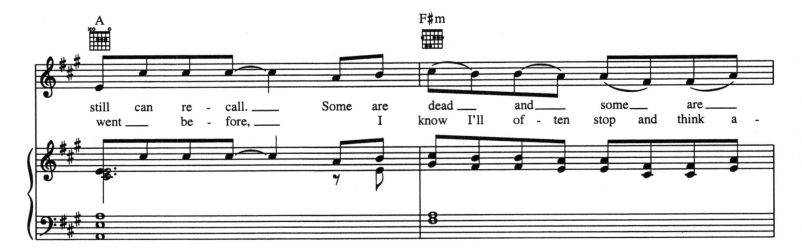

still can re - call.____ Some are dead___ and____ some___ are____
went ____ be - fore, ____ I know I'll of - ten stop and think a -

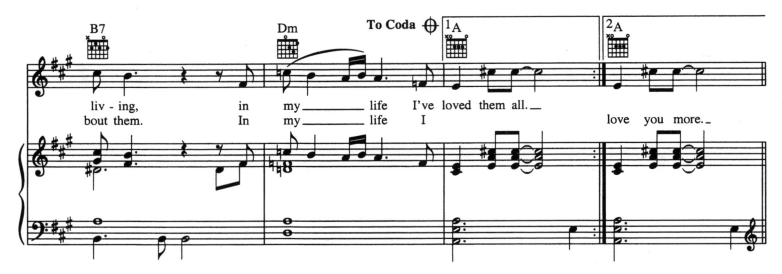

liv - ing, in my_____ life I've loved them all.__
bout them. In my_____ life I love you more.__

N.C.

in 18th century style

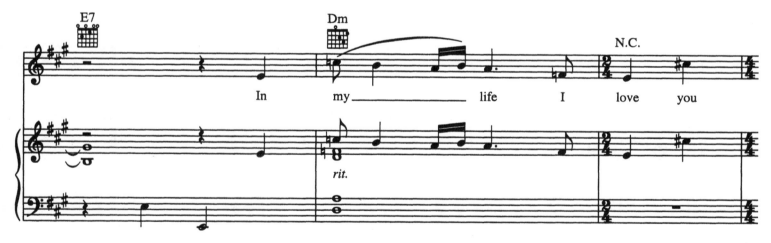

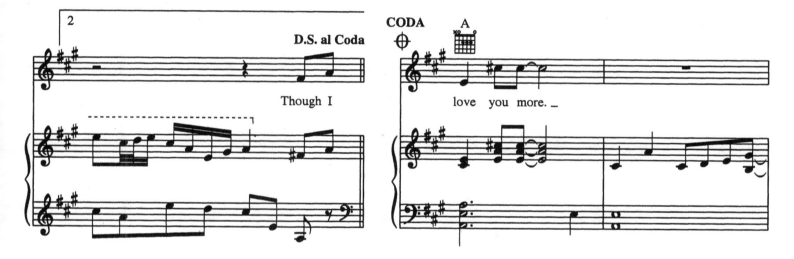

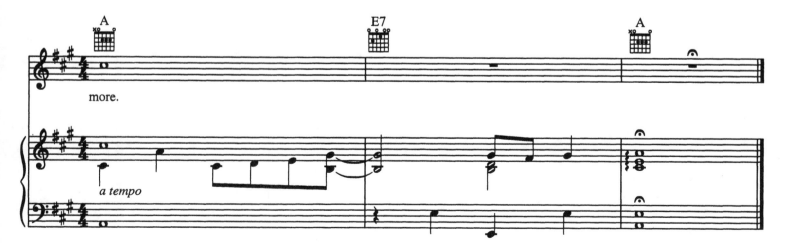

IT NEVER RAINS
(In Southern California)

Words and Music by ALBERT HAMMOND
and MICHAEL HAZELWOOD

Got on board __ a west __ bound sev - en __ for - ty sev -

- en, _____ did - n't think __ be - fore __ de - cid -

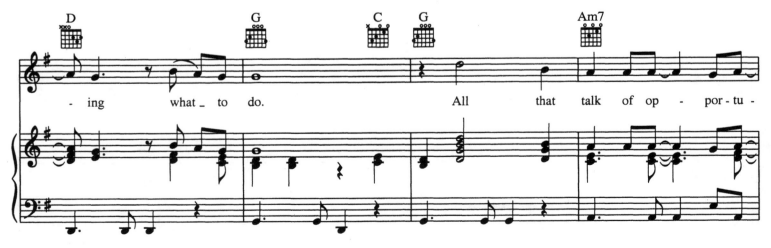

- ing what __ to do. All that talk of op - por - tu -

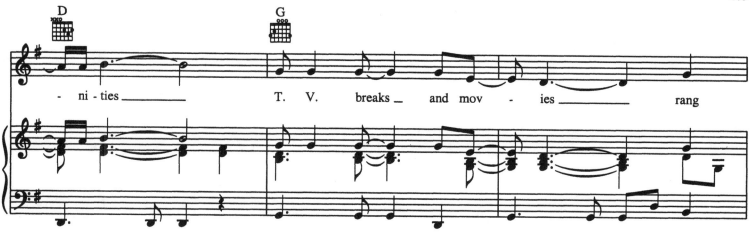

-ni-ties _____ T. V. breaks _ and mov - ies _____ rang

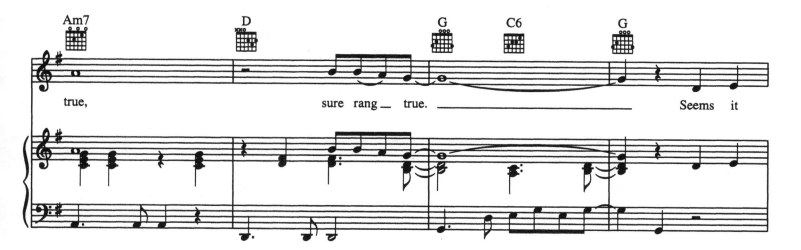

true, sure rang _ true. _____ Seems it

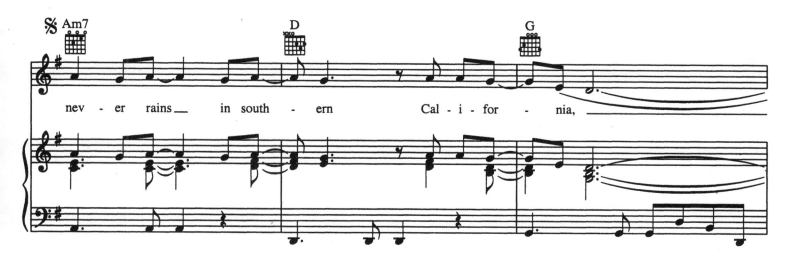

nev - er rains _ in south - ern Cal - i - for - nia, _____

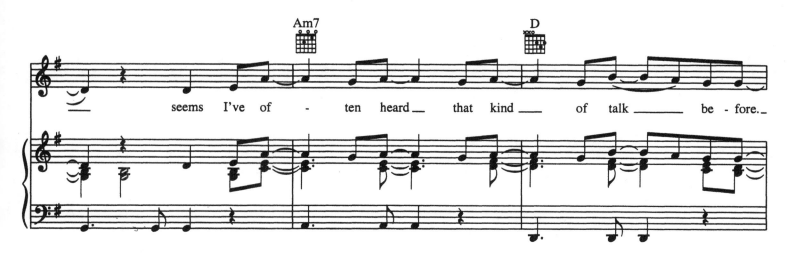

_ seems I've of - ten heard _ that kind _ of talk _ be - fore.

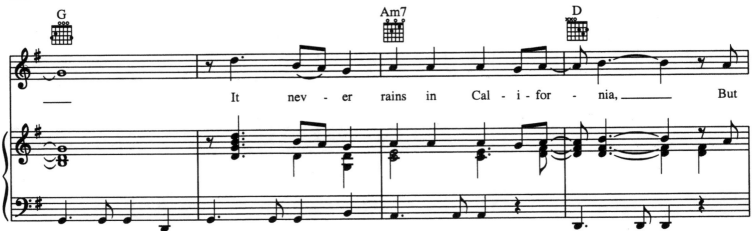

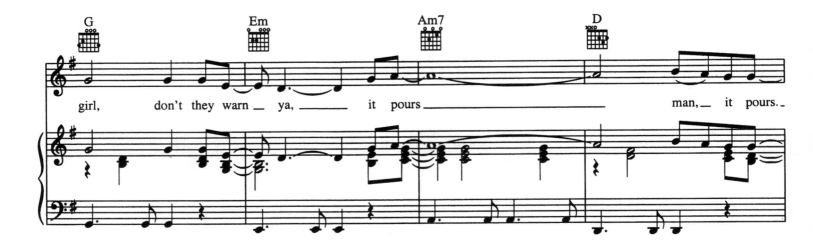

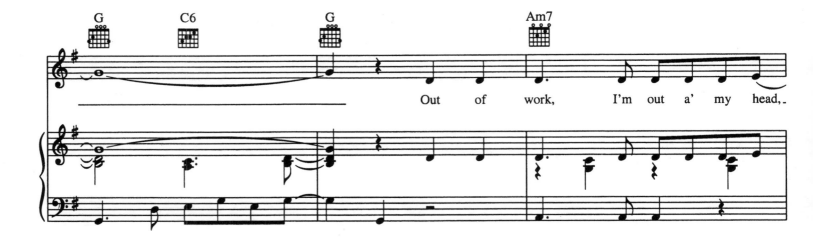

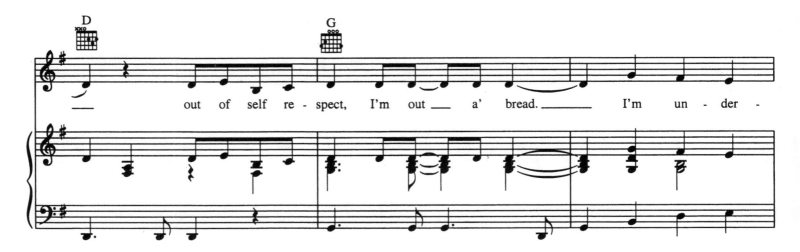

loved, I'm un - der - fed. _____ I wan - na go home. It nev - er

rains in Cal - i - for - nia, _____ but girl, don't they warn _

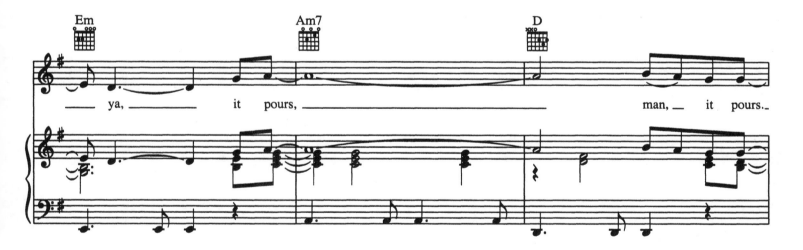

_____ ya, _____ it pours, _____ man, _ it pours._

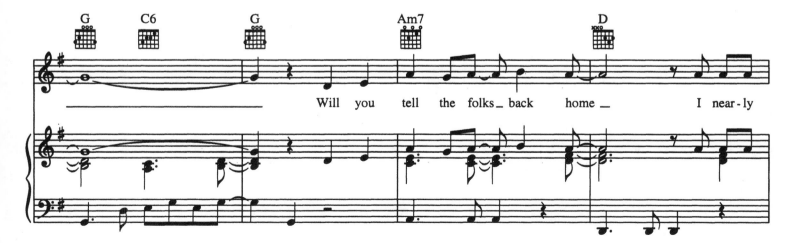

_____ Will you tell the folks _ back home _ I near - ly

made it, _____ had of - fers but __ don't __

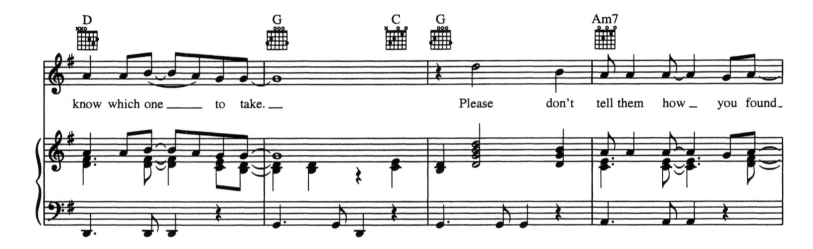

know which one _____ to take. __ Please don't tell them how _ you found _

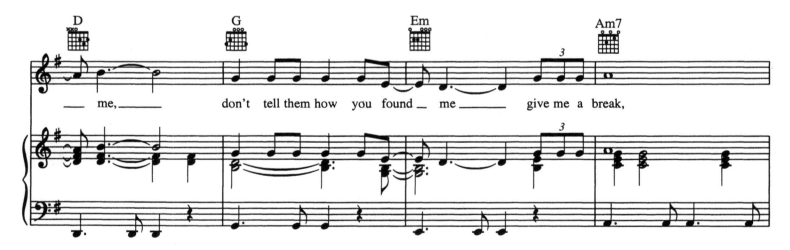

_ me, _____ don't tell them how you found _ me _____ give me a break,

D.S. and Fade | **Optional Ending**

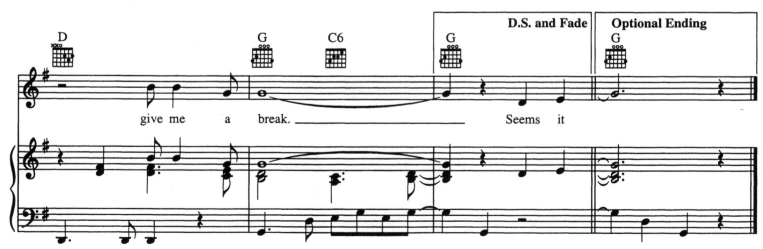

give me a break. _____ Seems it

LONGER

Words and Music by
DAN FOGELBERG

Long - er than__ there've been fish - es in the o - cean,
Strong - er than__ an - y moun - tain cath - e - dral.
Through the years__ as the fi - re starts to mel - low,

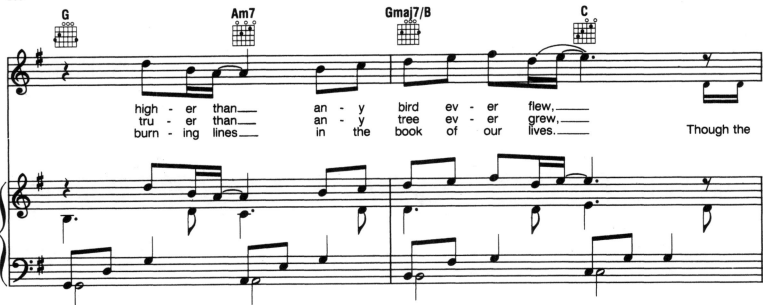

high - er than____ an - y bird ev - er flew,____
tru - er than____ an - y tree ev - er grew,____
burn - ing lines____ in the book of our lives.____

Though the

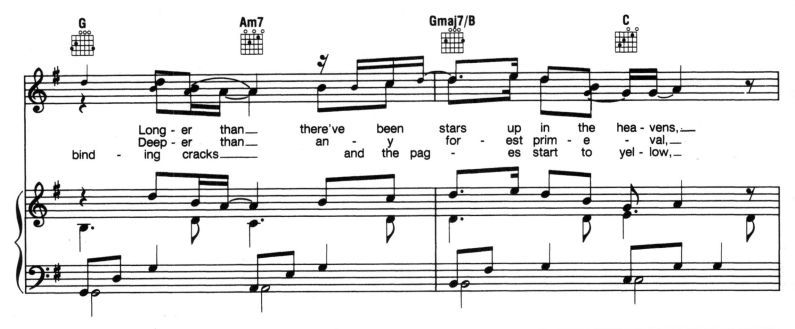

Long - er than____ there've been stars up in the hea - vens,____
Deep - er than____ an - y for - est prime - e - val,____
bind - ing cracks____ and the pag - es start to yel - low,____

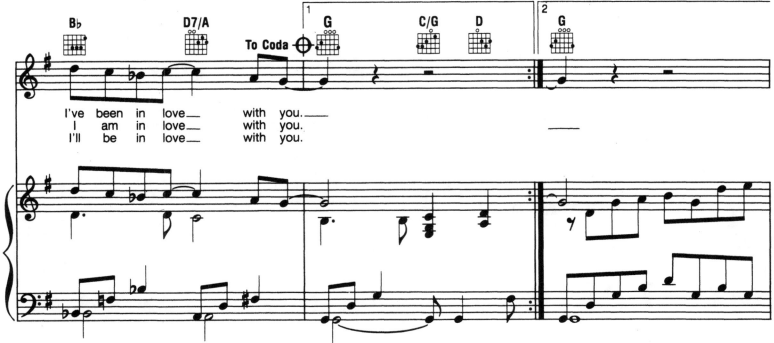

I've been in love____ with you.____
I am in love____ with you.
I'll be in love____ with you.

110

111

IT'S TOO LATE

Words by TONI STERN
Music by CAROLE KING

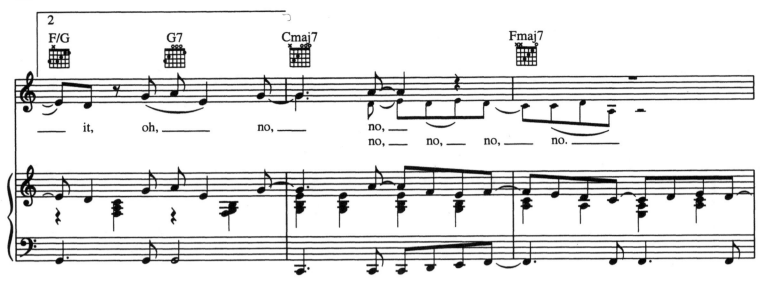

it, oh, _____ no, _____ no, _____
no, __ no, __ no, _____ no. _____

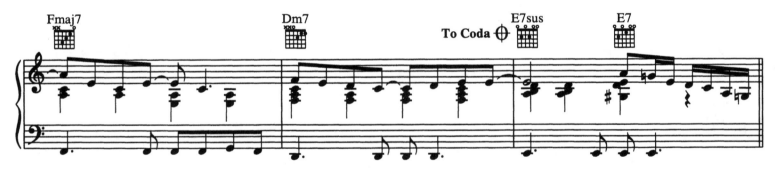

There'll be good times _ a-gain for me and _ you, ___ but we just can't stay to-geth - er; don't you

LOOK WHAT YOU'VE DONE TO ME

Words and Music by BOZ SCAGGS
and DAVID FOSTER

Love,

look what you've

LOVE SNEAKIN' UP ON YOU

Words and Music by JIMMY SCOTT
and TOM SNOW

122

up on you. Hey, _____ yeah.

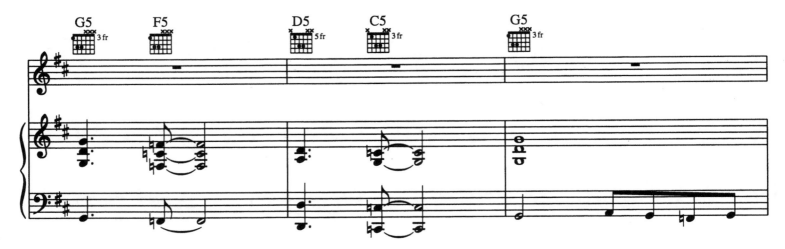

D.S. al Coda

CODA

up on you. _ Well, _____

125

MAKE IT WITH YOU

Words and Music by
DAVID GATES

Life,_____ it's for us to_____ keep.
Love_____ can be right or_____ wrong.___
Life,_____ it's for us to_____ keep.__

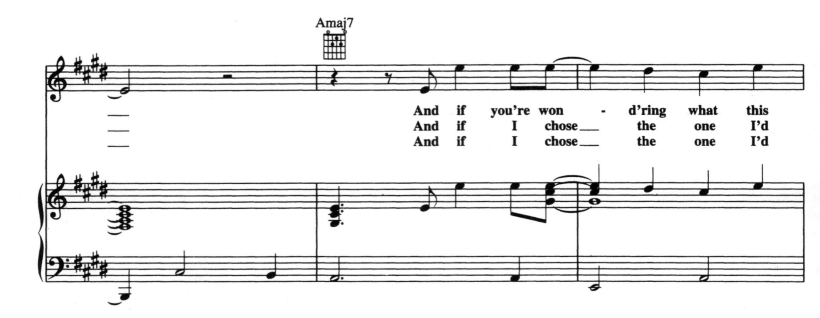

And if you're won - d'ring what this
And if I chose___ the one I'd
And if I chose___ the one I'd

all is lead - ing to,_____
like to help me through,_____
like to help me through,_____

I want to make____ it with you.____
I'd like to make____ it with you.____
I'd like to make____ it with you.____

I real - ly think _

that we____ could make __ it, girl. _____

MAMA TOLD ME
(Not to Come)

Words and Music by
RANDY NEWMAN

With a heavy beat

G7

Will you have whis-key with your wa-ter, or su-gar with your tea? What are
O-pen up the win-dow, let some air in-to this room.

these cra-zy ques-tions that you're ask-ing of me? This is
think I'm al-most cho-kin' on the smell of stale per-fume, and the

the wild-est par-ty that there ev-er could be. Oh don't turn on the lights 'cause I don't
cig-ar-ette you're smo-king 'bout to scare me half to death. Oh o-pen up the win-dow let me

THE M.T.A.

Words and Music by JACQUELINE STEINER
and BESS HAWES

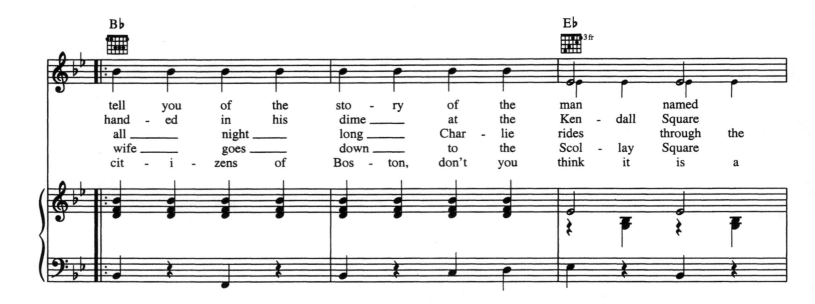

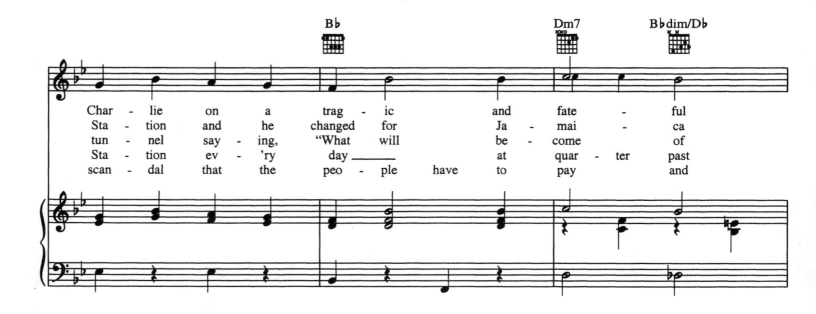

day. \
Plain. \
me? \
two. \
pay?

He put ten cents in his \
When he got there, the con - \
How can I af - \
And through the o - pen \
Fight the fare in -

pock - et, kissed his wife and fam - 'ly, went to \
duc - tor told him, "One more nick - el." Char - lie \
ford to see my sis - ter in Chel - sea, or my \
win - dow she hands Char - lie a sand - wich as the \
crease, Fight the fare in - crease, get

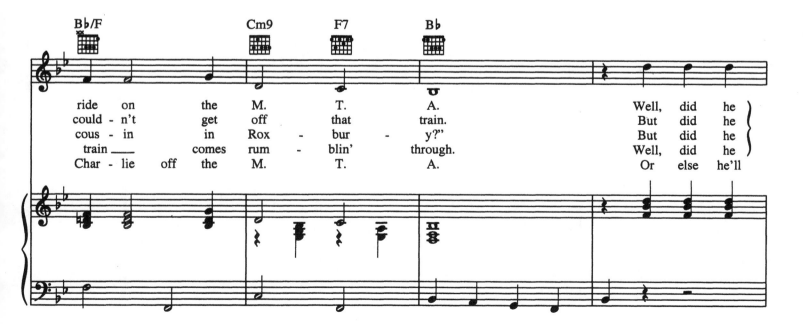

ride on the M. T. A. Well, did he \
could - n't get off that train. But did he \
cous - in in Rox - bur - y?" But did he \
train comes rum - blin' through. Well, did he \
Char - lie off the M. T. A. Or else he'll

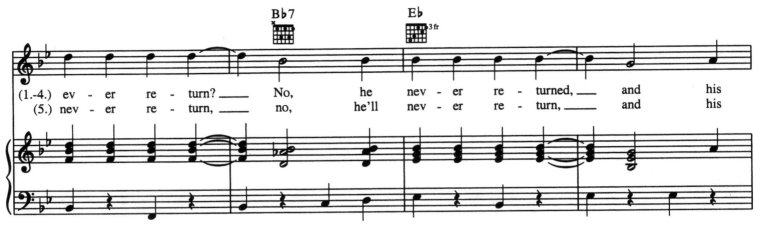

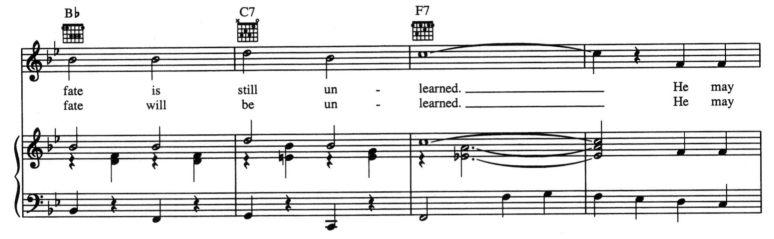

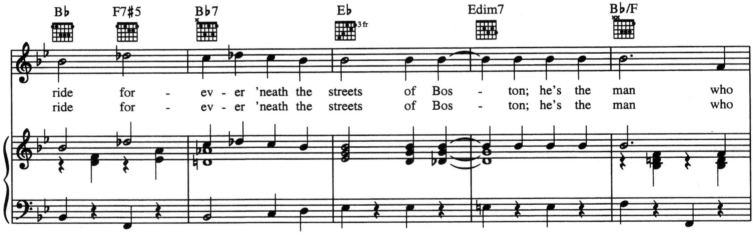

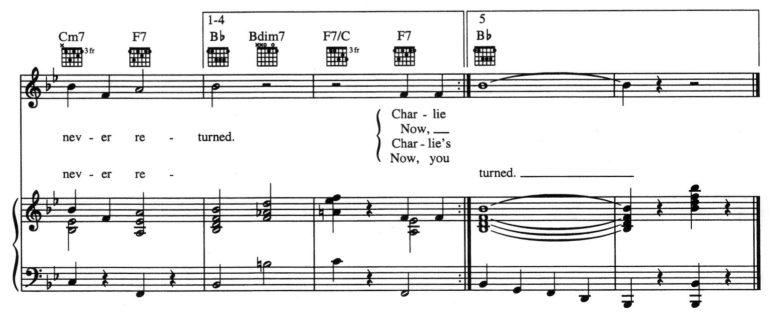

RIDE LIKE THE WIND

Words and Music by
CHRISTOPHER CROSS

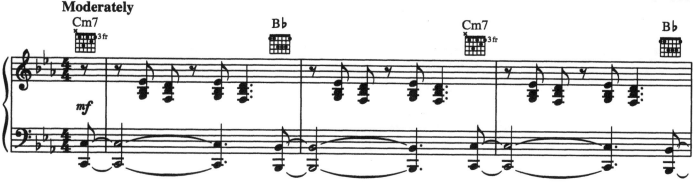

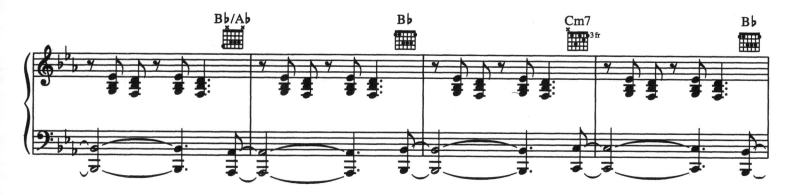

It is the night. My bod-y's weak. I'm on the run. No time for sleep.

I've got to ride, ride like the wind to be free a-gain.

And I've got ___ such a long __ way to go ___ to

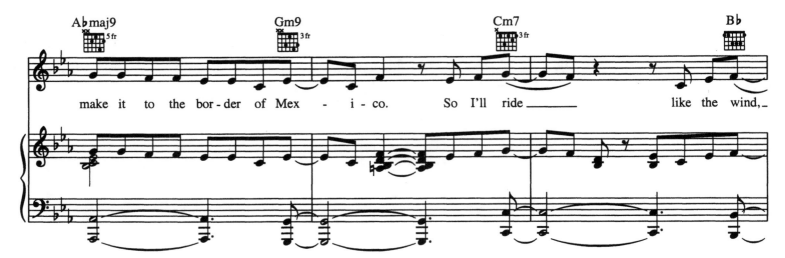

make it to the bor-der of Mex - i - co. So I'll ride ____ like the wind, _

To Coda ⊕

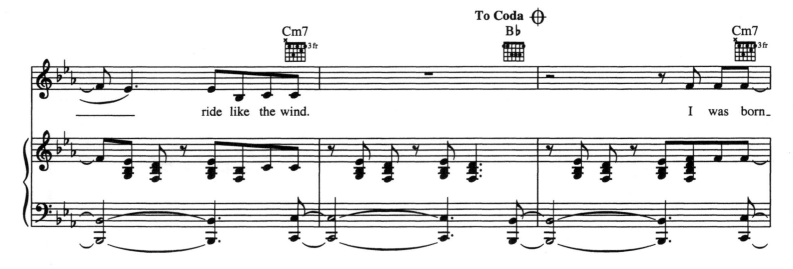

____ ride like the wind. I was born _

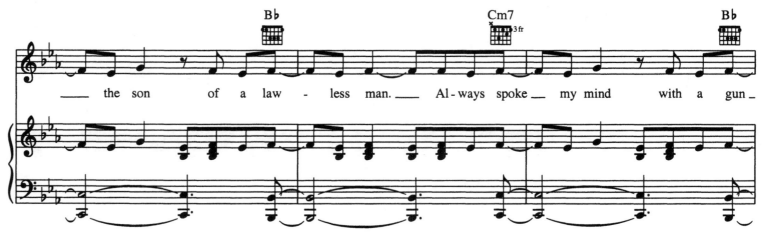

_ the son of a law - less man. _ Al-ways spoke _ my mind with a gun _

139

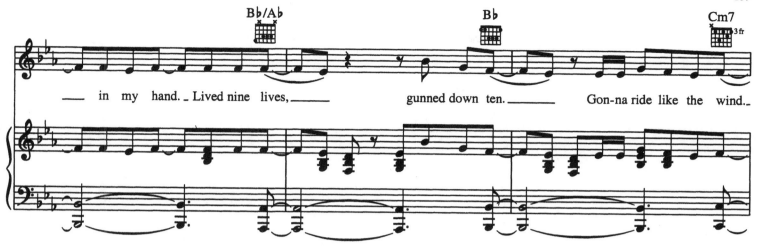

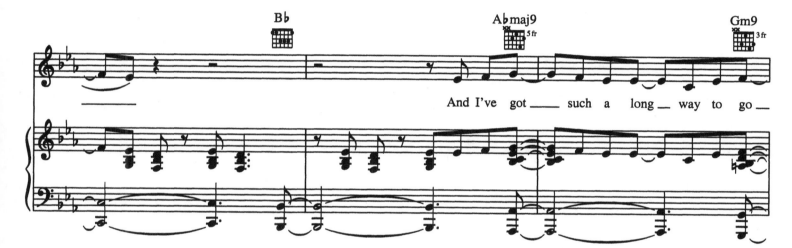

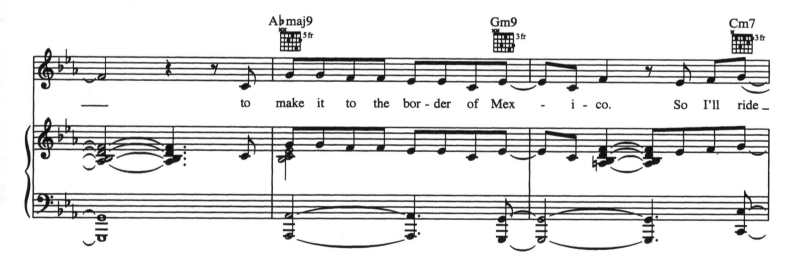

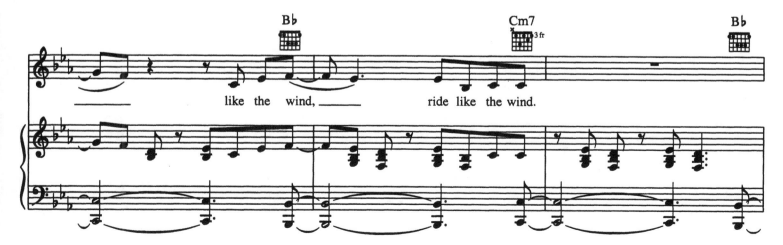

140

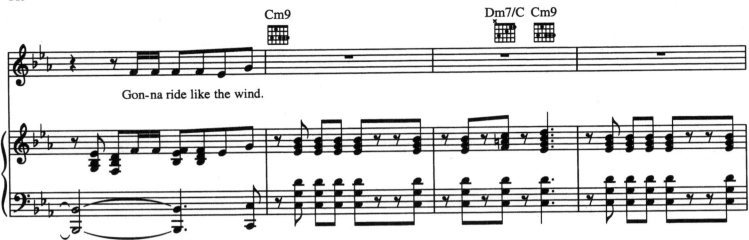

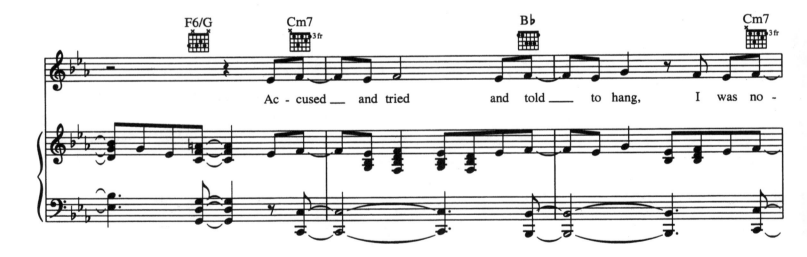

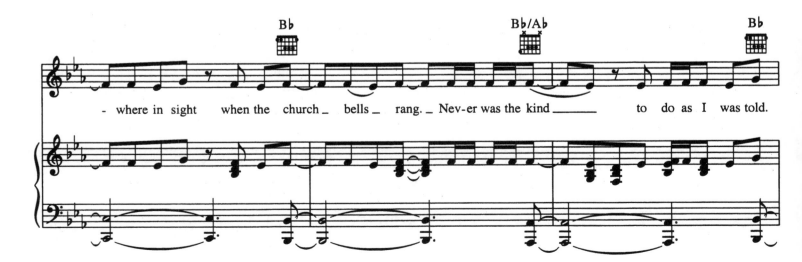

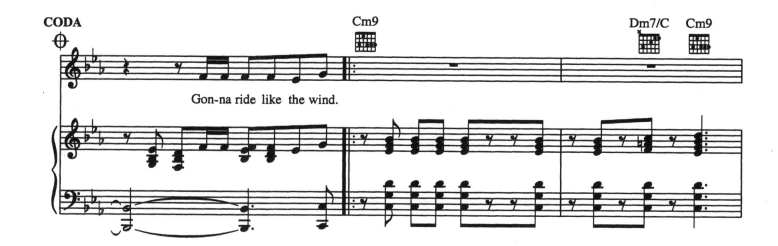

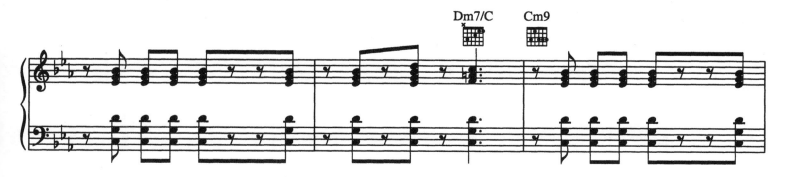

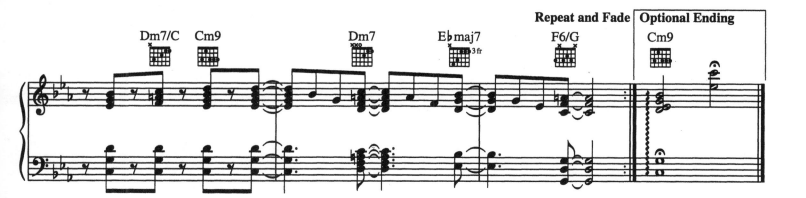

NEW YORK STATE OF MIND

Words and Music by
BILLY JOEL

the Dai - ly News _____

D.S. *for verse 3 & 5*

mind _____

OUR HOUSE

Words and Music by
GRAHAM NASH

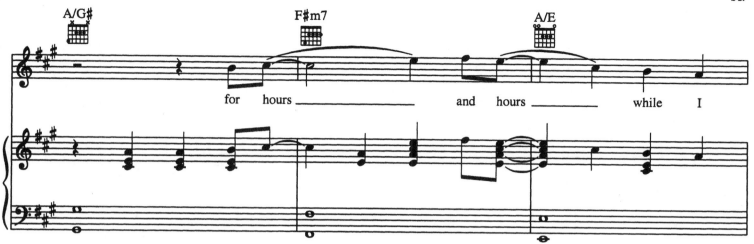

for hours _____ and hours _____ while I

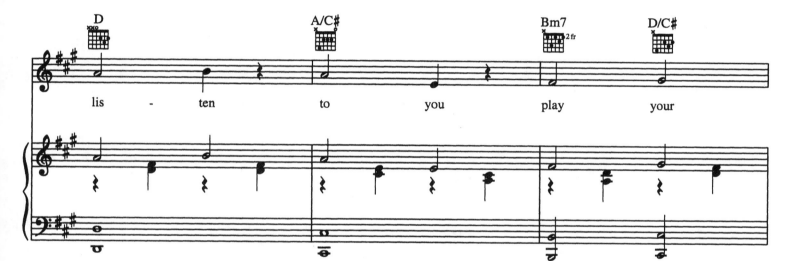

lis - ten to you play your

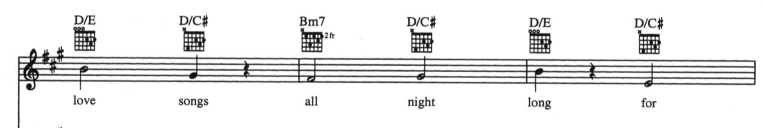

love songs all night long for

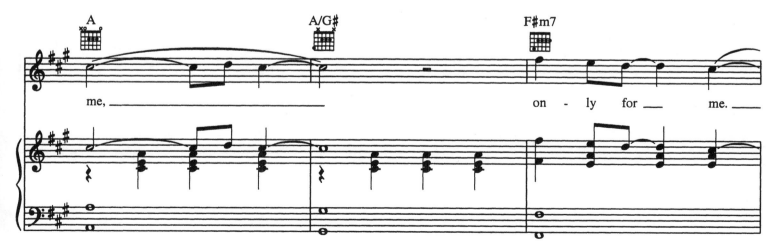

me, _____ on - ly for ___ me. _____

148

The win - dows are il - lu - mi - nat - ed
(Such a co - zy room.) ___

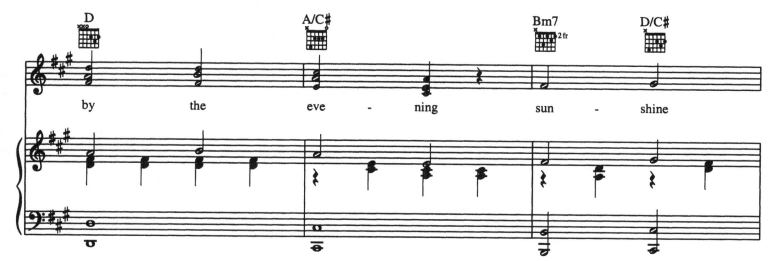

by the eve - ning sun - shine

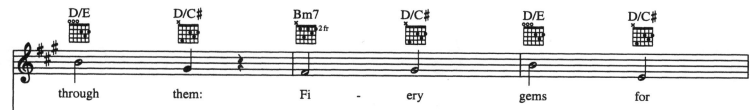

through them: Fi - ery gems for

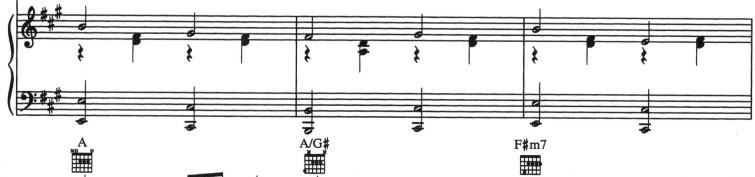

you, ___ on - ly for ___ you. ___

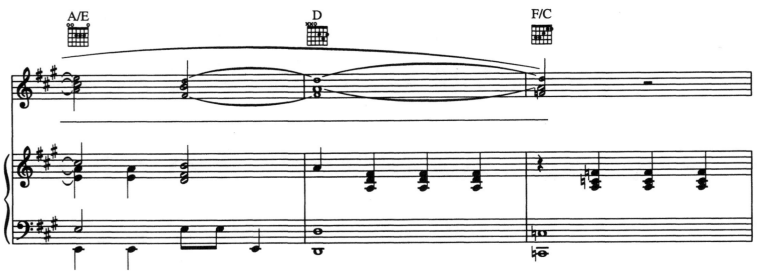

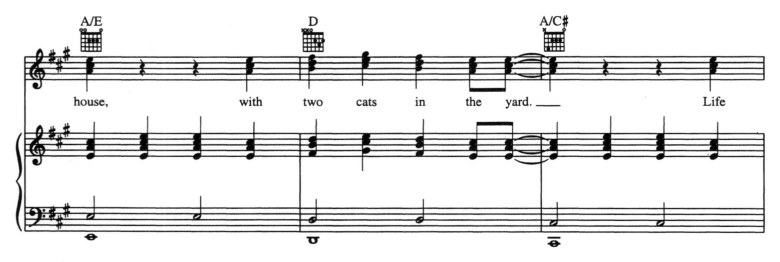

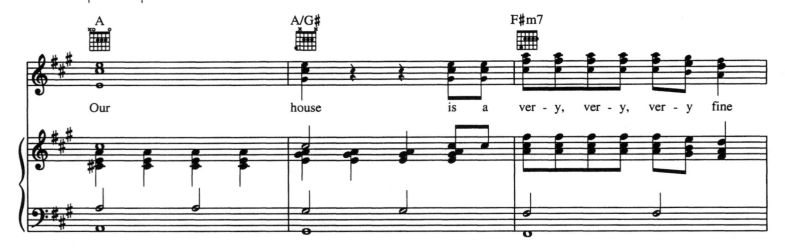

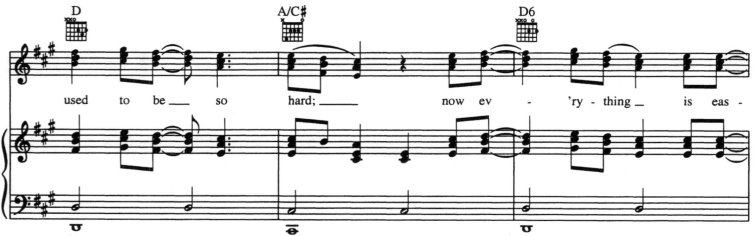

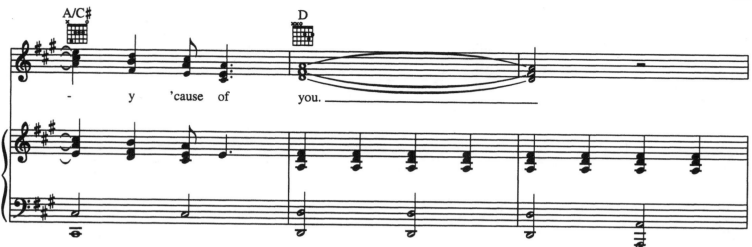

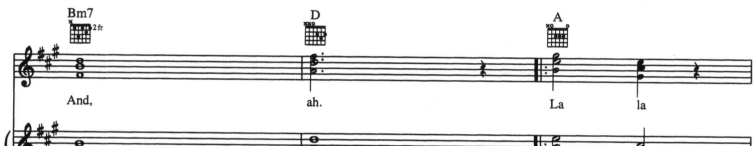

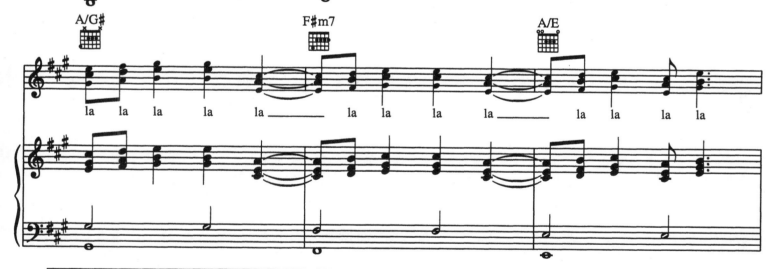

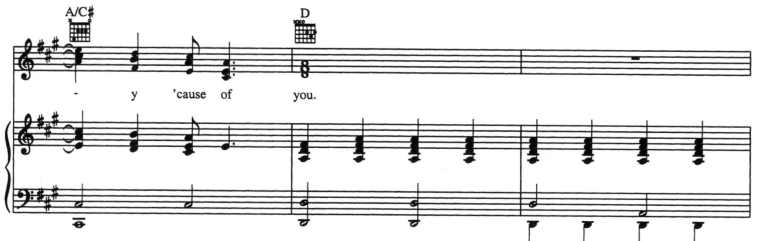

-y 'cause of you.

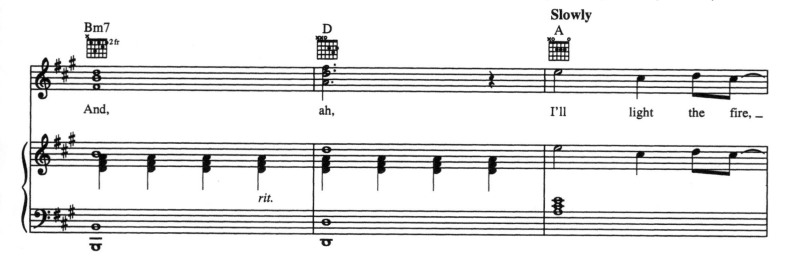

And, ah, I'll light the fire,

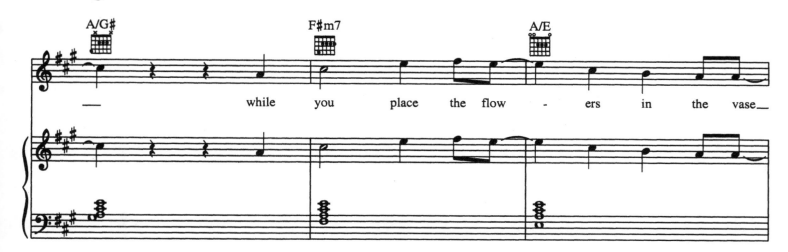

while you place the flow - ers in the vase

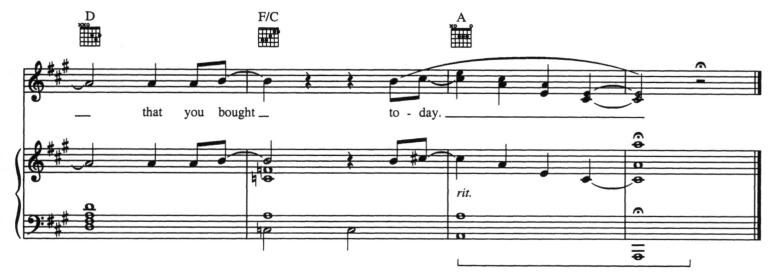

that you bought to - day.

SAN FRANCISCO BAY BLUES

Words and Music by
JESSE FULLER

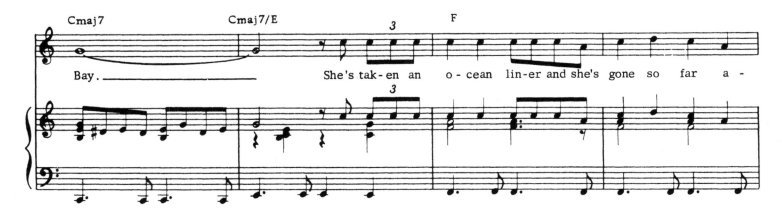

I'm gon-na lay down and die. _____ I have-n't got a nick-el, Ain't got a lous-y

dime, _____ If she don't come back, I think I'm gon-na lose my mind, _____

— If she ev-er comes back to stay, There's gon-na be an-oth-er brand new day__

— Walk-in' with my Ba-by down by the San Fran-cis-co Bay. _____

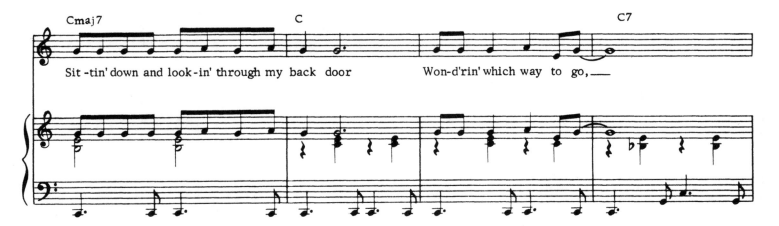

Sit-tin' down and look-in' through my back door Won-d'rin' which way to go, ___

Wo-man I'm so cra-zy 'bout she don't want me no more.

Think I'll take me a freight train, Be-cause I'm feel-in' blue,

Ride all the way to the end of the line, __ Think-in' on-ly of you.

157

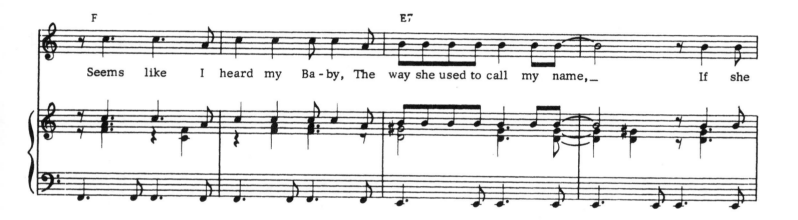

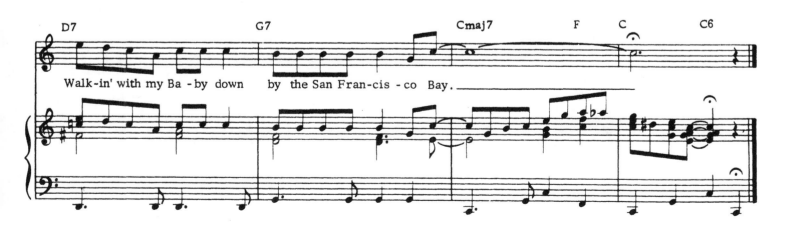

A SATISFIED MIND

Words and Music by JOE "RED" HAYES
and JACK RHODES

Moderately slow

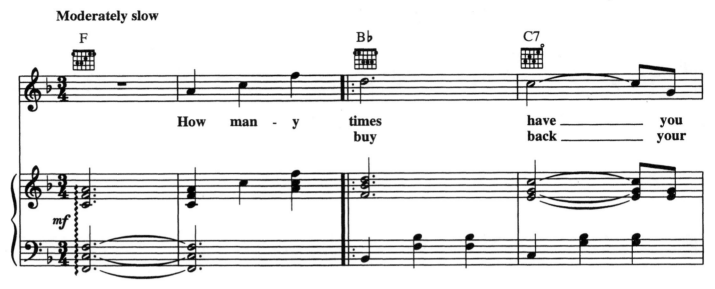

How man-y times have ___ you
buy back ___ your

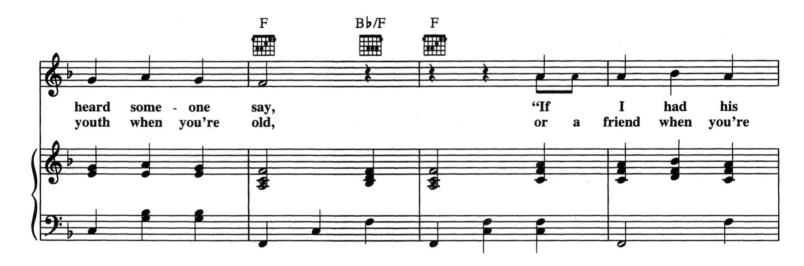

heard some-one say,
youth when you're old,

"If I had his
or a friend when you're

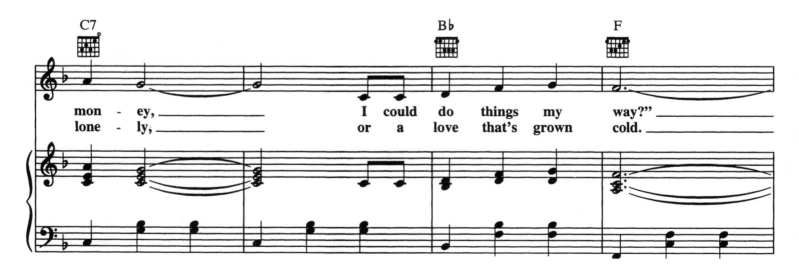

mon-ey, ___
lone-ly; ___

I could do things my way?"
or a love that's grown cold.

159

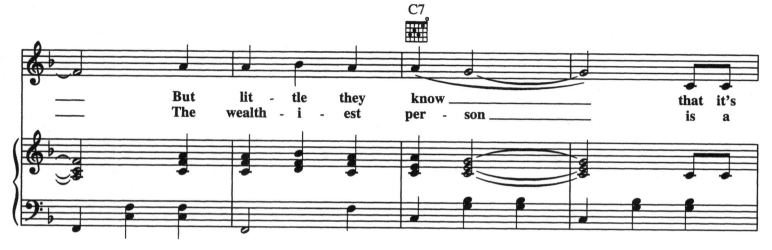

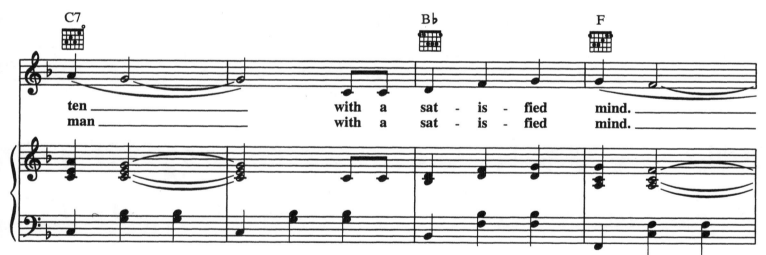

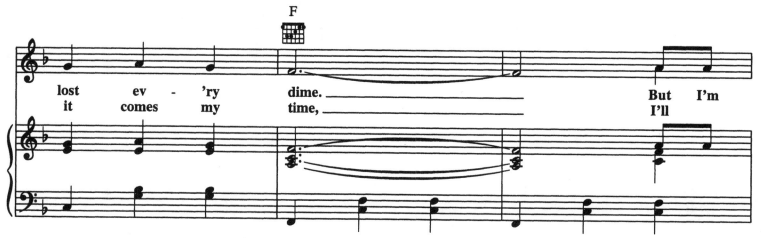

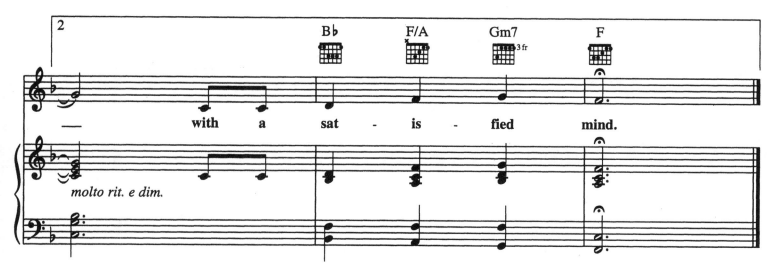

SILVER THREADS
AND GOLDEN NEEDLES

Words and Music by DICK REYNOLDS
and JACK RHODES

SOMETHING TO TALK ABOUT

(Let's Give Them Something to Talk About)

Words and Music by
SHIRLEY EIKHARD

Moderate Reggae/Rock

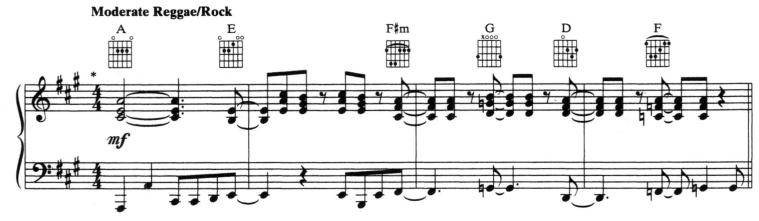

Peo - ple are talk - ing, talk - ing a - bout peo - ple.___
I feel so fool - ish. I nev - er no - ticed that,___

I hear them whis - per, you won't___ be - lieve it.
ba - by, you're act - ing so nerv - ous, like___ you're fall - ing.

* Recorded a half step lower

Let's ____ give them some-thing to talk ____ a - bout. ____ Let's give them ____ some-thing to
Come on, give them some-thing to talk ____ a - bout, ____ a lit - tle ____ mys - t'ry to

talk a - bout. ____ I wan-na give them some-thing to talk a - bout. ____ I want your love. ____
fig - ure out. ____

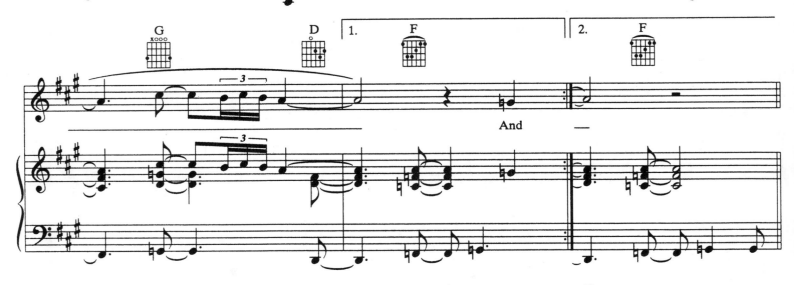

And ____

Give a lit-tle some-thing to talk a - bout,_____ babe._____ I got some mys- t'ry, why don't

you just fig- ure out._____ Give them some - thing to talk a - bout. How a - bout

love?_____ Wooh,_____

lis-ten up, ba-by.   A lit-tle mys-t'ry won't hurt.___

Give them some-thing to talk a-bout. How a-bout___ love?___

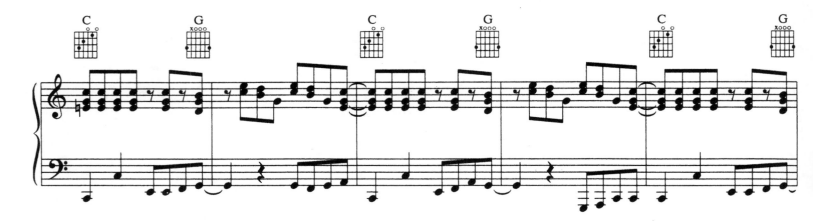

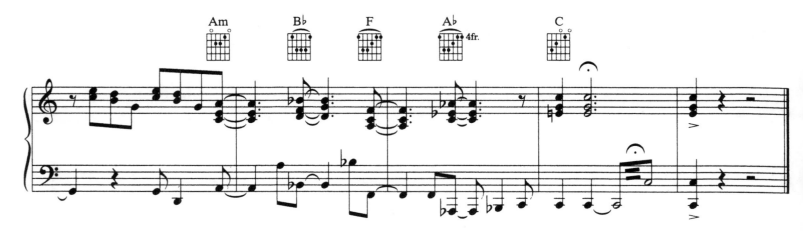

SUMMER IN THE CITY

Words and Music by JOHN SEBASTIAN,
STEVE BOONE and MARK SEBASTIAN

sum - mer_____ in the cit - y._____

sum - mer_____ in the cit - y._____

(Instrumental)

D.S. and Fade
(Instrumental)

SUNSHINE ON MY SHOULDERS

Words by JOHN DENVER
Music by JOHN DENVER, MIKE TAYLOR and DICK KNISS

TRAVELIN' MAN

Words and Music by
JERRY FULLER

Moderately

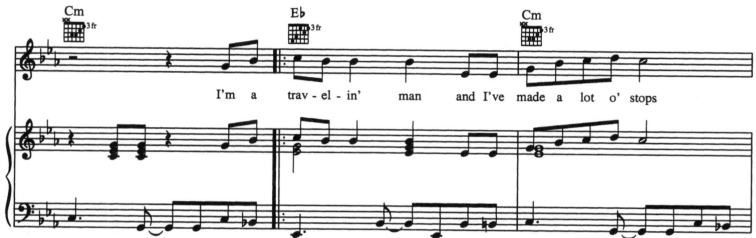

I'm a trav-el-in' man and I've made a lot o' stops

all o-ver the world; and in ev-er-y port I

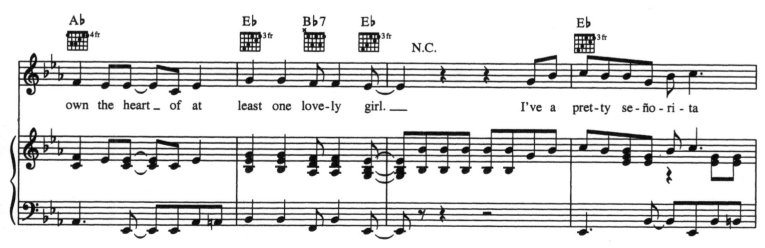

own the heart of at least one love-ly girl. I've a pret-ty se-ño-ri-ta

wait-in' for me ___ down in old Mex - i - co; ___ and if you're

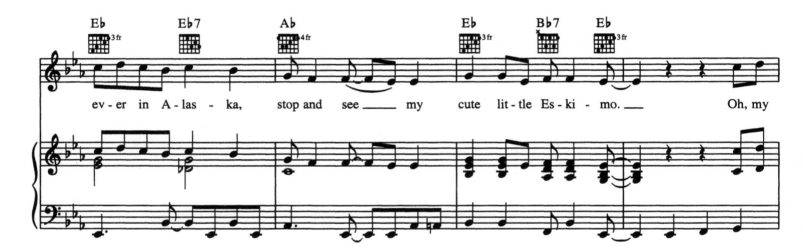

ev - er in A-las - ka, stop and see ___ my cute lit-tle Es-ki - mo. ___ Oh, my

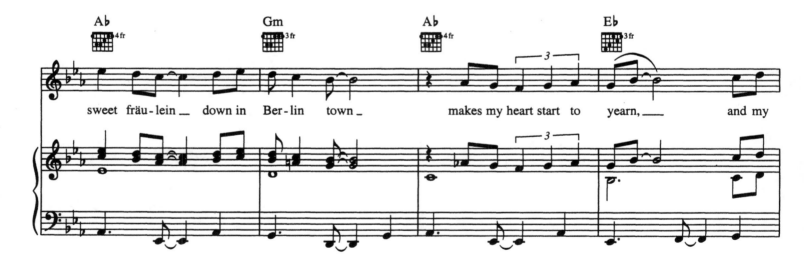

sweet fräu-lein ___ down in Ber-lin town ___ makes my heart start to yearn, ___ and my

Chi - na doll ___ down in old Hong Kong waits for my re -

turn. Pret - ty Pol - y - ne - sian ba - by o - ver the sea, ___

I re - mem - ber the night ___ when we walked on the sands of

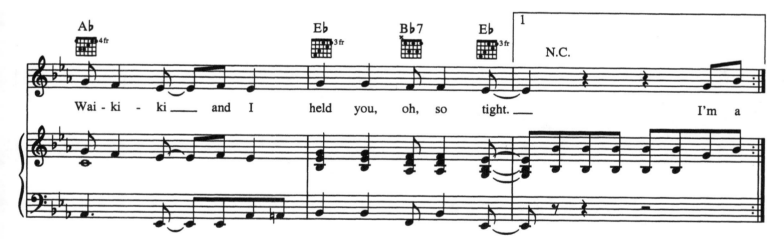

Wai - ki - ki ___ and I held you, oh, so tight. ___ I'm a

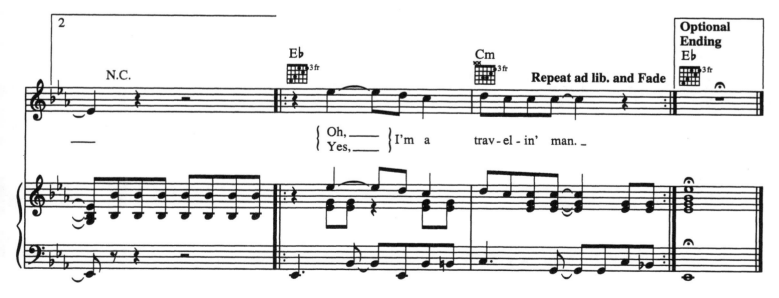

{ Oh, ___ } I'm a trav - el - in' man. _
{ Yes, ___ }

THIS LAND IS YOUR LAND

Words and Music by
WOODY GUTHRIE

1. This land is

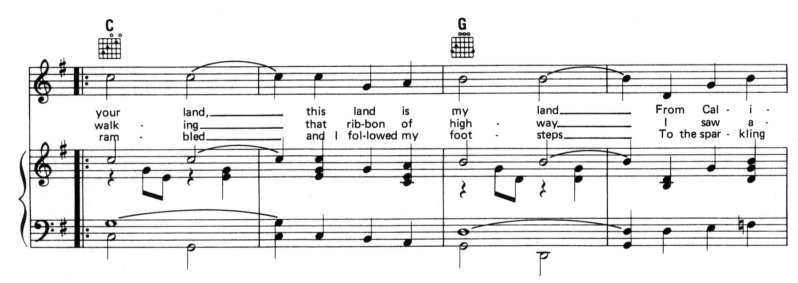

your land,_____ this land is my land_____ From Cal-i-
walk - ing_____ that rib-bon of high - way_____ I saw a-
ram - bled_____ and I fol-lowed my foot - steps_____ To the spar - kling

for - nia_____ to the New York is - land,_____ From the red - wood
bove me_____ that end - less sky - way;_____ I saw be-
sands of her dia - mond des - erts;_____ And all a-

4. When the sun came shining, and I was strolling,
And the wheat fields waving and the dust clouds rolling,
As the fog was lifting a voice was chanting:
This land was made for you and me.

5. As I went walking, I saw a sign there,
And on the sign it said "No Trespassing."
But on the other side it didn't say nothing,
That side was made for you and me.

6. In the shadow of the steeple I saw my people,
By the relief office I seen my people;
As they stood there hungry, I stood there asking
Is this land made for you and me?

7. Nobody living can ever stop me,
As I go walking that freedom highway;
Nobody living can ever make me turn back,
This land was made for you and me.

THOSE WERE THE DAYS

Words and Music by
GENE RASKIN

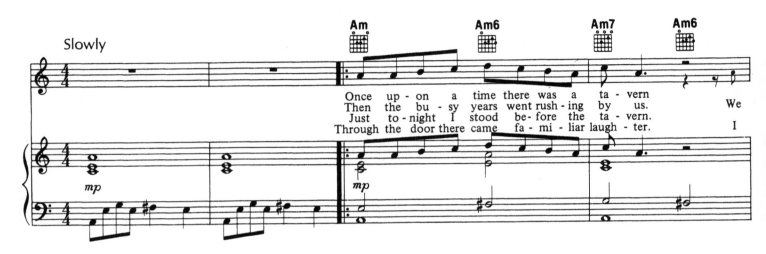

Slowly

Once up-on a time there was a ta-vern
Then the bu-sy years went rush-ing by us. We
Just to-night I stood be-fore the ta-vern. I
Through the door there came fa-mi-liar laugh-ter.

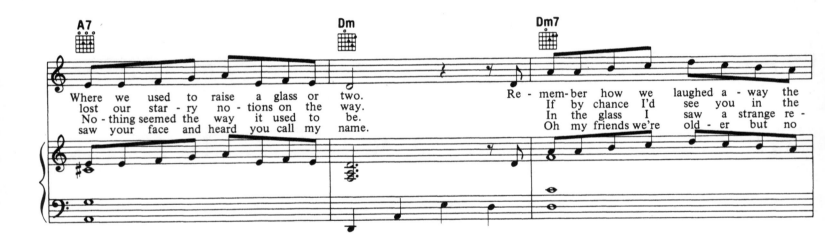

Where we used to raise a glass or two.
lost our star-ry no-tions on the way.
No-thing seemed the way it used to be.
saw your face and heard you call my name.

Re-mem-ber how we laughed a-way the
If by chance I'd see you in the
In the glass I saw a strange re-
Oh my friends we're old-er but no

hours,— And dreamed of all the great things we would do. Those Were The
ta-vern, We'd smile at one an-oth-er and we'd say - Those Were The
flec-tion, Was that lone-ly fel-low real-ly me? Those Were The
wis-er, For in our hearts the dreams are still the same. Those Were The

TIME IN A BOTTLE

Words and Music by
JIM CROCE

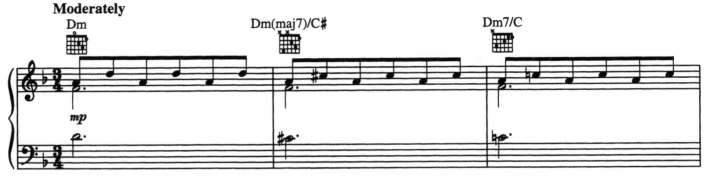

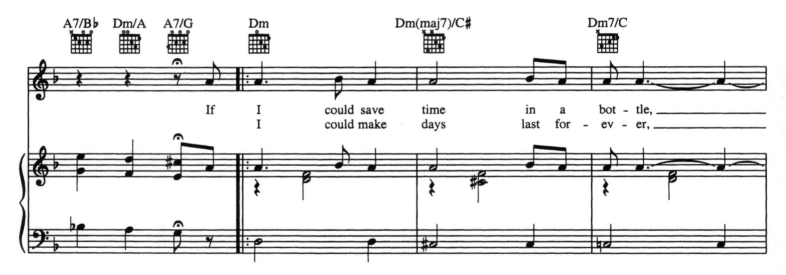

If I could save time in a bot - tle, _____

I could make days last for - ev - er, _____

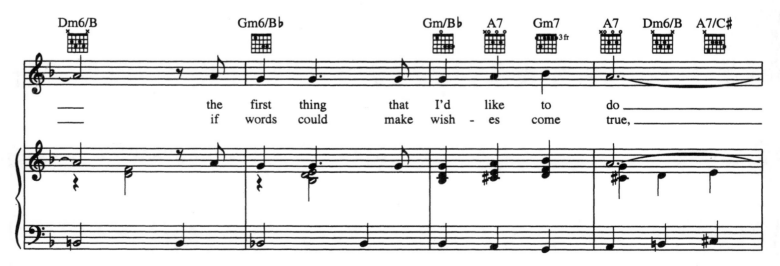

the first thing that I'd like to do _____

if words could make wish - es come true, _____

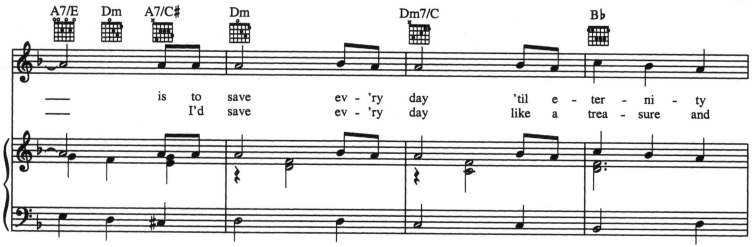

is to save ev - 'ry day 'til e - ter - ni - ty
I'd save ev - 'ry day like a trea - sure and

pass - es a - way just to spend them with you.
then a - gain I would spend them with you.

If But there nev - er seems to

be e - nough time to do the things you want to do once you

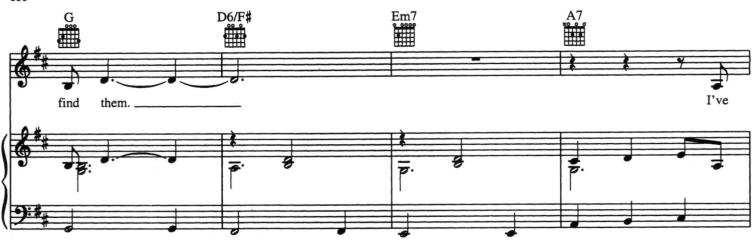

find them. _____ I've

looked a-round e-nough to know that you're the one I want to go through

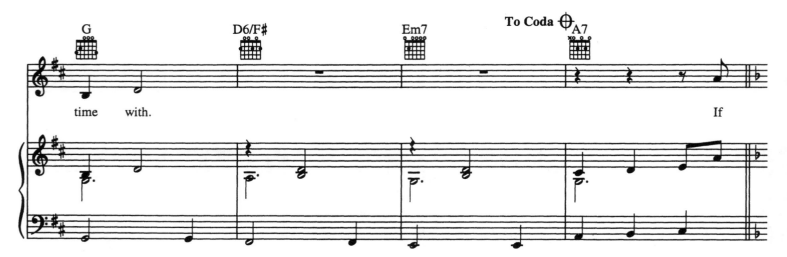

time with. If

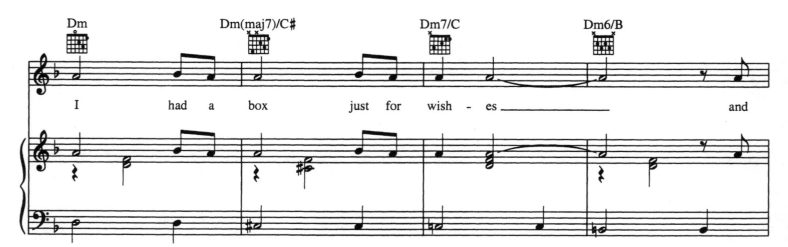

I had a box just for wish-es _____ and

187

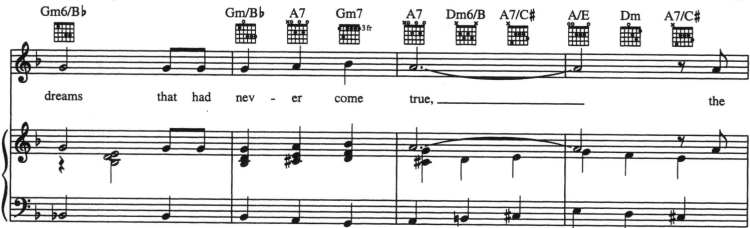

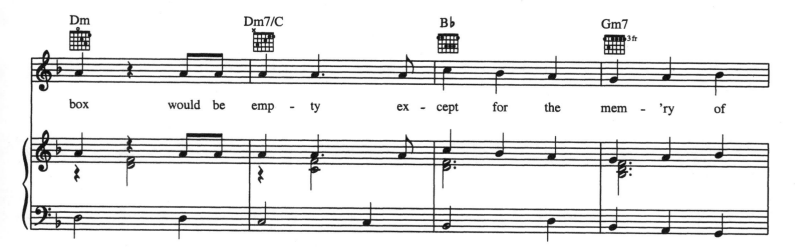

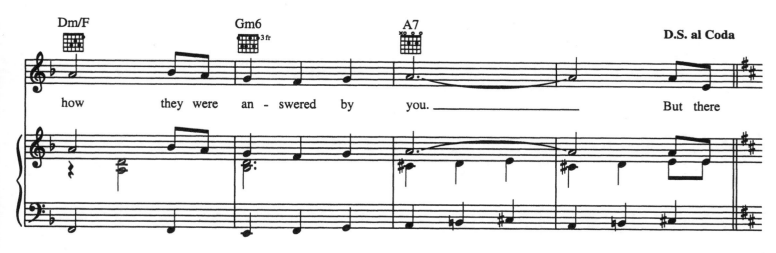

TURN AROUND

Words and Music by ALAN GREENE,
MALVINA REYNOLDS and HARRY BELAFONTE

Moderately, with much feeling

Where are you going, my little one,
Where are you going, my little one,
little one? Where are you going, my
little one? Little dirndls and petticoats,
baby, my own? Turn around and you're
where have you gone? Turn around and you're

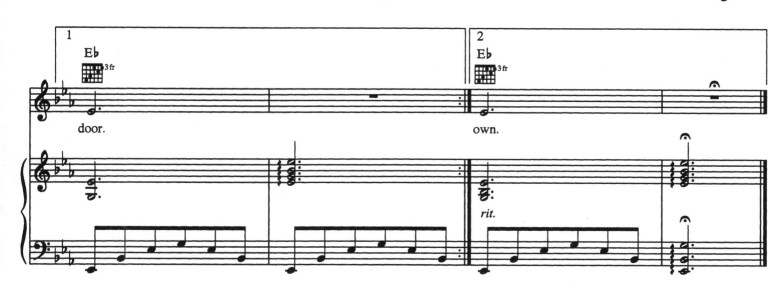

TURN! TURN! TURN!
(To Everything There Is a Season)

Words from the Book of Ecclesiastes
Adaptation and Music by PETE SEEGER

THE UNICORN

Words and Music by
SHEL SILVERSTEIN

2. Lord seen some sinnin' and it caused him pain,
   He says, "Stand back, I'm gonna make it rain.
   So hey, Brother Noah, I'll tell you what to do,
   Go and build me a floating zoo."
CHORUS:
   "And you take two alligators and a couple of geese,
   Two hump back camels and two chimpanzees,
   Two cats, two rats, two elephants, but sure as you're born,
   Noah, don't you forget my unicorns."

3. Now Noah was there and he answered the callin'
   And he finished up the ark as the rain started fallin',
   Then he marched in the animals two by two,
   And he sung out as they went through:
CHORUS:
   "Hey Lord, I got you two alligators and a couple of geese,
   Two hump back camels and two chimpanzees,
   Two cats, two rats, two elephants, but sure as you're born,
   Lord, I just don't see your unicorns."

4. Well, Noah looked out through the drivin' rain,
   But the unicorns was hidin'— playin' silly games,
   They were kickin' and a-splashin' while the rain was pourin',
   Oh them foolish unicorns.
CHORUS: Repeat 2nd Chorus

5. Then the ducks started duckin' and the snakes started snakin',
   And the elephants started elephantin' and the boat started shakin',
   The mice started squeakin' and the lions started roarin',
   And everyone's aboard but them unicorns.
CHORUS:
   I mean the two alligators and a couple of geese,
   The hump back camels and the chimpanzees,
   Noah cried, "Close the door 'cause the rain is pourin',
   And we just can't wait for them unicorns."

6. And then the ark started movin' and it drifted with the tide
   And the unicorns looked up from the rock and cried,
   And the water came up and sort of floated them away,
   That's why you've never seen a unicorn to this day.
CHORUS:
   You'll see a lot of alligators and a whole mess of geese,
   You'll see hump back camels and chimpanzees,
   You'll see cats and rats and elephants but sure as you're born,
   You're never gonna see no unicorn.

UNTIL IT'S TIME FOR YOU TO GO

Words and Music by
BUFFY SAINTE-MARIE

Slow Waltz

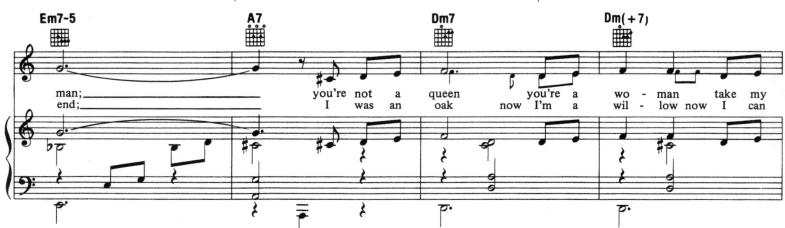

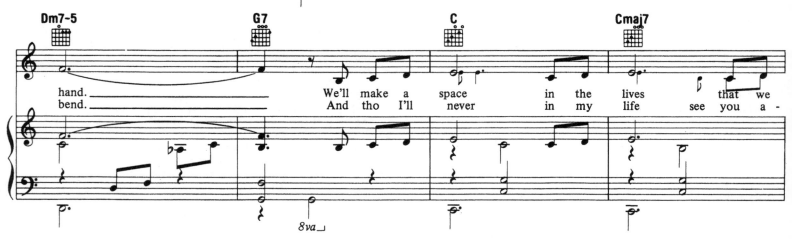

WE'RE ALL ALONE

Words and Music by
BOZ SCAGGS

200

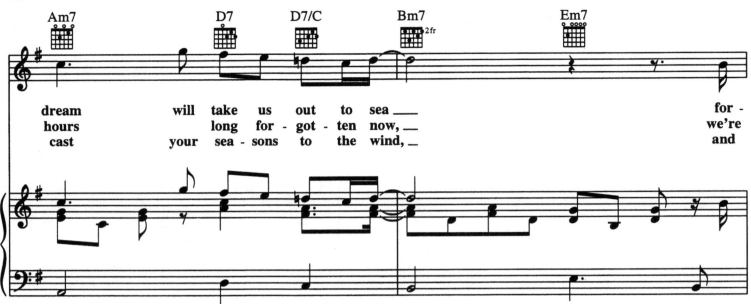

dream   will take us   out to sea ___   for -
hours   long for - got - ten now, ___   we're
cast   your sea - sons to the wind, ___   and

ev - er - more, _____   for - ev - er - more. __
all a - lone, _____   we're all a - lone. __
hold me, dear, _____   oh, hold me, dear. __

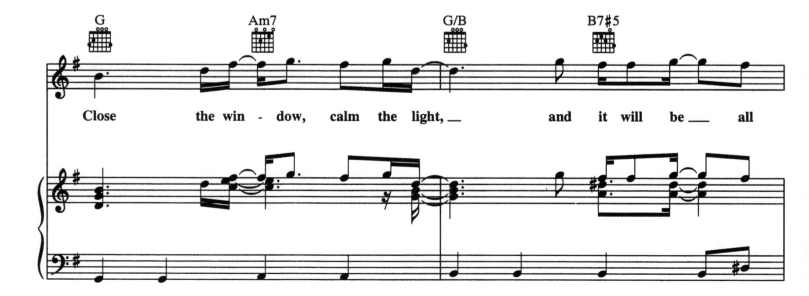

Close   the win - dow, calm the light, __   and it will be ___ all

201

WALK RIGHT IN

Words and Music by GUS CANNON
and H. WOODS

Slowly, with strong beat

1. Walk Right In, _____ set right _____ down, _____ Dad - dy, let your mind roll _____
2. Walk Right In, _____ set right _____ down, _____ Ba - by, let your hair hang _____

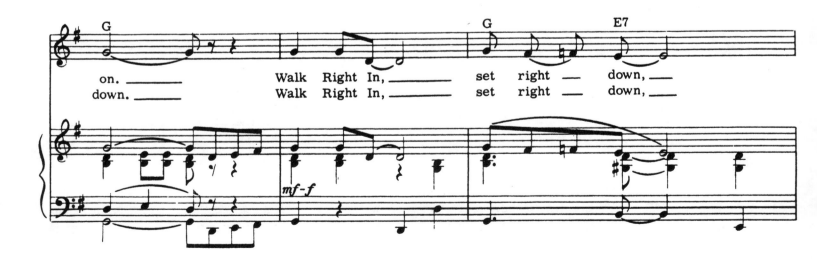

on. _____ Walk Right In, _____ set right _____ down, _____
down. _____ Walk Right In, _____ set right _____ down,

WE'LL SING IN THE SUNSHINE

Words and Music by
GALE GARNETT

WEDDING BELL BLUES

Words and Music by
LAURA NYRO

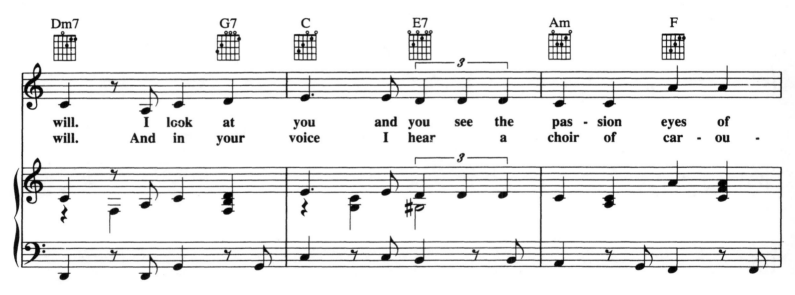

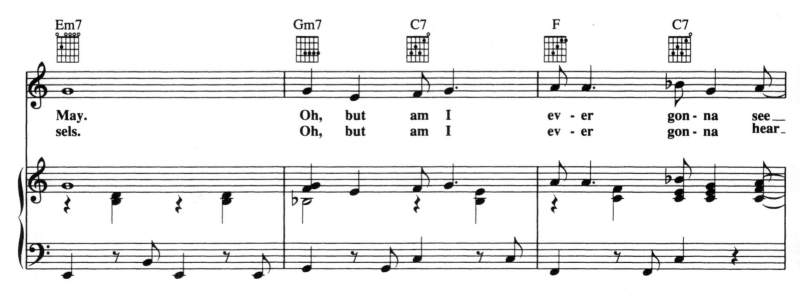

209

A WHITER SHADE OF PALE

Words and Music by KEITH REID
and GARY BROOKER

211

YELLOW DAYS

English Lyric by ALAN BERNSTEIN
Music and Spanish Lyric by ALVARO CARRILLO

With An Easy Flow

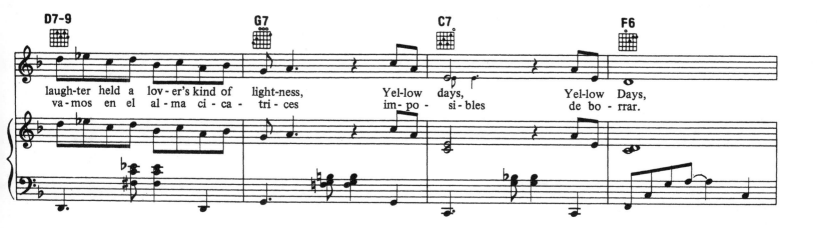

She would hold me and a smile would spread a - round us so com -
Se te ol - vi - da que has - ta pue - do ha - cer - te mal si me de -

plete - ly, And the soft - ness of a kiss would lin - ger sweet - ly. Yel - low
ci - do pues tu a - mor lo ten - go muy com - pro - me - ti - do pe - ro a

Days, Yel - low Days._____ But then came thun - der and I
fuer - za no se - rá._____ Y hoy re - sul - ta que no

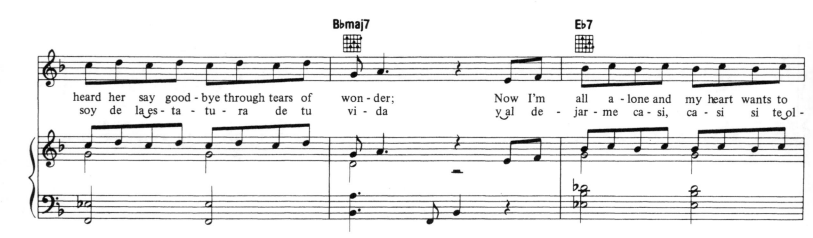

heard her say good - bye through tears of won - der; Now I'm all a - lone and my heart wants to
soy de la es - ta - tu - ra de tu vi - da y al de - jar - me ca - si, ca - si si te ol -

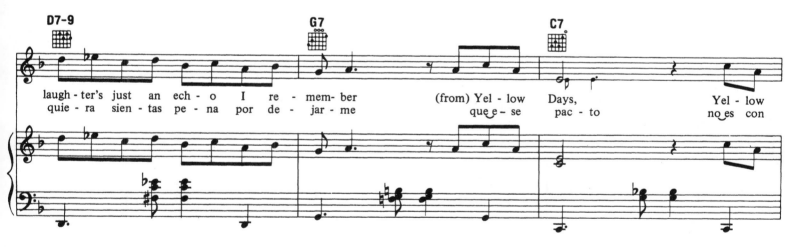

YOU DIDN'T HAVE TO BE SO NICE

Words and Music by JOHN SEBASTIAN
and STEVE BOONE

YOU'VE GOT A FRIEND

Words and Music by
CAROLE KING

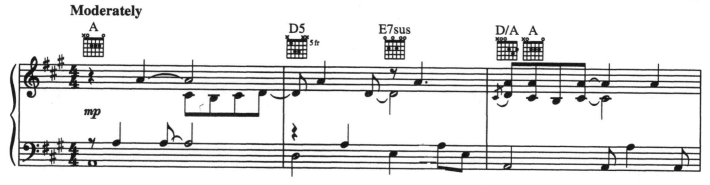

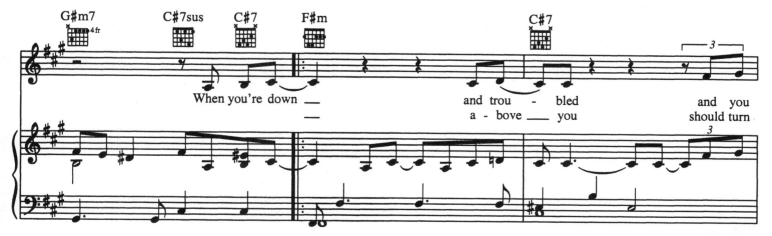

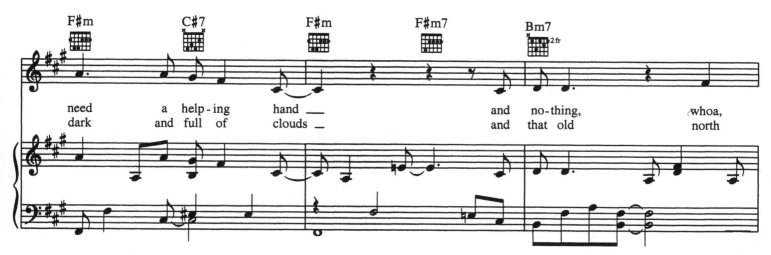

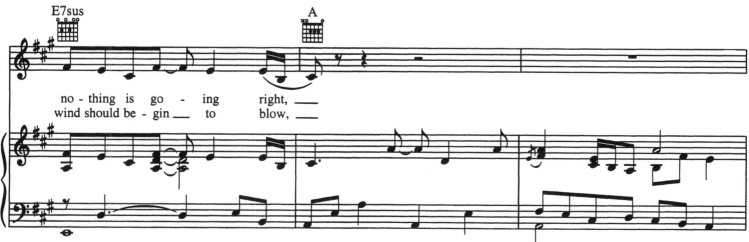

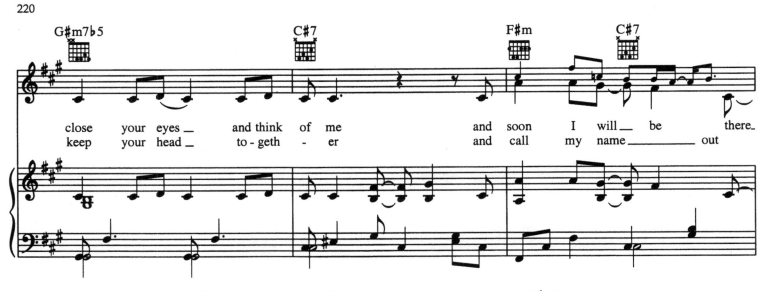

close your eyes __ and think of me and soon I will __ be there __
keep your head __ to - geth - er and call my name _____ out

__ loud, _____ now; __ to bright-en up e - ven your dark - est night __
soon I'll be knock - ing up-on __ your door. __

You just call ____ out my name,__

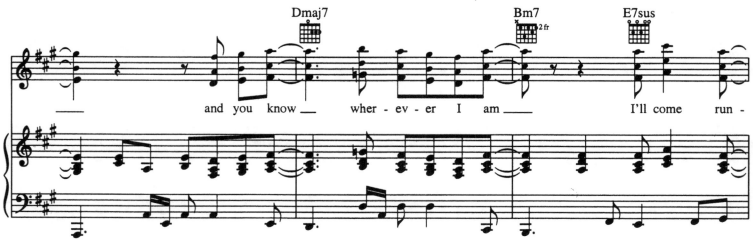

and you know ___ wher - ev - er I am ___ I'll come run -

*Vocal harmony sung 2nd time only

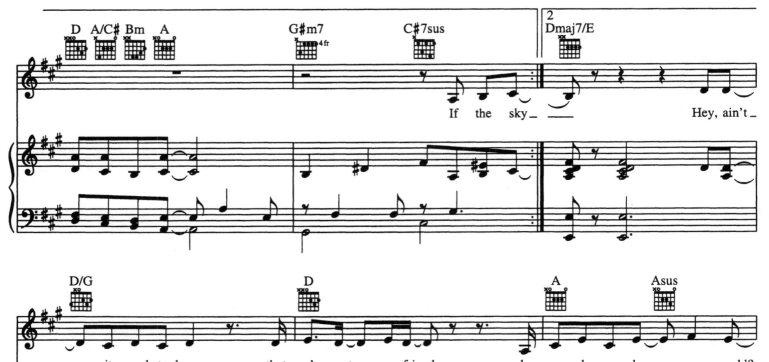

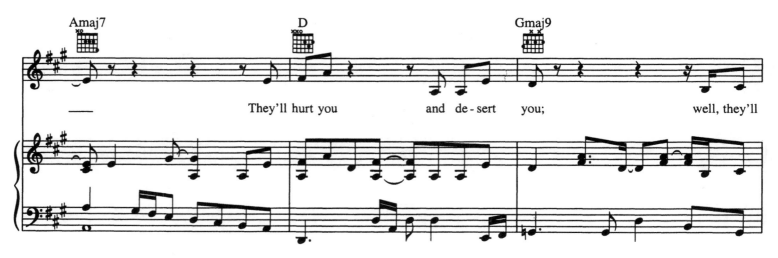

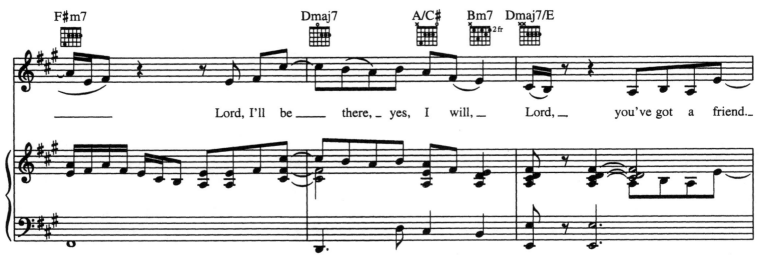